AF240904

ANGUISH

Max Dorra

ANGUISH

Max Milo

Max Milo Editions, Paris, 2023
www.maxmilo.com
ISBN : 978-2-31501-143-8

"We are simply
anxiety illiterates."
Günther Anders, *The Obsolescence of Man.*

"Does he have any *life-changing* secrets? No, he's
just looking for them," I replied.
Arthur Rimbaud, *A Season in Hell.*

Introduction - Starting from an oversight

"Soul", "spirit", "psyche", whatever the term used to designate this elusive entity, the only thing certain is that it can suffer. To this pain which is not physical, psychiatry proposes remedies, philosophy systems. Most often, however, these disciplines seem to miss the point. A blindness, an oblivion which, invaded as it is by stereotypes, everyday life does not escape either. This curious absence has a significance, a meaning. This book will try to approach it.

Psychiatry and the forgetfulness of the singular

Psychiatry is a territory that begins with the opening of bodies and ends with the opening of dreams. From Bichat to Freud.

The complaints that the autopsy does not explain, nor the X-rays or the magnetic resonance, the sufferings that escape the medical glance, psychiatry collects them and, for lack of understanding them, classifies them.

When Freud, on July 24, 1895, interpreted one of his dreams by applying the method of free association, he was able to reveal to the psychiatry of his time what had escaped him: the place, unconscious, of childhood. The virtual world of *memory*.

Later, anti-psychiatry reminded psychiatry and psychoanalysis of the field that the singularity of a being was inexorably confronted with: that of social realities.

In 1951, Laborit, a surgeon and neurobiologist, discovered the effects of chlorpromazine. At that time, molecules acting on anxiety, depression and delirium gradually came on the scene. However, as with any medication, these products had to be tested on "homogeneous groups of patients". Hence the use of computers. The hegemony of the mathematical model in the "human sciences" found a spectacular and dramatic illustration in the *Diagnostic and Statistical Manual of Mental Disorders*, the DSM, which was revised periodically[1], a collective work of

---

1. DSM-IV-TR - *Diagnostic and Statistical Manual of Mental Disorders*, Masson, Paris, 2004. It would be unfair not to point

the American Psychiatric Association, which became the official international manual of psychiatry. It includes information on "how to score the Global Assessment of Functioning (GFA)". To code a case of bipolar disorder (or manic-depressive psychosis), for example, one can choose between 296.0x, 296.40, 294.4x, 296.6x, 296.5x, 296.7, 296.89, depending on the date and severity of the most recent manic or depressive episode. One can imagine what can happen when listening to a patient is parasitized by the need for such a number. The worst part, as Allen Frances says, is that "the diagnosis will change both *the way the individual sees himself* and the way others see him[2]".

---

out the precautions taken by the authors of the book in their "Introduction": "The text of the DSM-IV (as previously in the DSM-III-R) avoids the use of terms such as 'a schizophrenic' or 'an alcoholic'. They are replaced by more precise - but admittedly more cumbersome - expressions such as "an individual with schizophrenia", or "an individual with alcohol dependence"." Phrases on which those who speak of "cancer patients" or "AIDS patients" could meditate. As we can see, nothing is simple. In May 2013, the DSM-V was published.

2. Allen Frances is the American psychiatrist who led the team that produced the DSM-IV. He also says: "The slightest extension or lowering of the threshold of a diagnosis is a boon to the pharmaceutical companies. Bipolar disorder type 2,

Thus, caught in the trap of its own discourse, psychiatry has gradually been transformed into an immense paradoxical injunction. It presents itself as a liberating discipline, while at the same time, by its very language, its classifying gaze, its diagnoses, its *evaluations*, it anguishes almost imperceptibly.

Philosophy and the oblivion of anguish

It is to forget their anguish that philosophers create concepts. Affectivity ("not very virile") has long been excluded from the field of philosophy, a discipline reserved for men for centuries.[3]

But everyone is afraid. A fear that goes back to childhood. This fear, very rare - the courageous - are those who dare to admit it, is an essential step however if one seeks to overcome it. All the more so

which we introduced, has allowed pharmaceutical companies, through television advertising in particular, to double the number of patients treated for bipolar disorder." See site: http://bibliobs.nouvelobs.com/en-partenariat-avec-books/20130329.OBS6215/allen-frances-la-psychiatrie-est-en-derapage-incontrole.html.

3. "The heart is a female organ. To treat it thus requires in the moral order a competence as particular as that of the gynecologist in the physiological order", Roland BARTHES, "Celle qui voit clair", in *Mythologies*, Éditions du Seuil, Paris, 1970, p. 125.

as each one, unaware of or denying the anguish of others, believes that he/she is the only one affected by what he/she thinks is an illness.

If the class struggle is the engine of history, the fuel of this engine is the anguish of individuals. This is something that no "society project" should ignore.

It is almost always the anguish that is hidden behind the violence. This is very difficult to imagine when one is the object of an aggression. The conversion of anguish into murderous hatred, however, is tragically illustrated in certain pages of *Mein Kampf...*[4]

---

4. "This was the time when the most profound revolution that I had ever had to carry out was made in me. The energetic cosmopolitan that I had been until then became a fanatical anti-Semite. Once again - but it was the last time - *a painful anguish gripped my heart.* As I studied the influence of the Jewish people through long periods of history, I suddenly wondered *anxiously* if fate did not intend, for reasons unknown to us poor men, the final victory of this little people? *If the Jew, with the help of his Marxist profession of faith, wins the victory over the peoples of this world, his diadem will be the funeral crown of humanity.* Then our planet will begin to travel through the ether again: there will be no more men on its surface. In defending myself against the Jew, I fight to defend the work of the Lord [...] November 1918: *in these nights hatred was born in me. With the Jew, there is no need to make a pact, but only to decide: all or nothing*", Adolf HITLER, *My Fight* (*Mein Kampf*, 1925), pp. 36-37 and pp. 105-107. See: https://

Kierkegaard, Sartre, not to mention Heidegger (whom Hitler did not worry about...), all evoke anguish but, contrary to Hegel, none of them, not even Lacan, eats it up.

Daily life and the forgetting of a hold, that of the groups

From morning to night, without always being aware of it, we are caught in groups. Their clichés, the stories, where we are assigned a stereotyped role. Groups which can be the best, but also the worst of things if we are not warned of the perils of *the therapeutic illusion* - anxiolytic - that they dispense. A hard drug, it can indeed lead to murderous mimicry, as the "group illusion" (Anzieu) is most often accompanied by a blind submission to authority. During Eichmann's trial, Arendt evoked "his horrible gift of consoling himself with clichés". In this, she joined Anzieu. But she could not have foreseen that, fifty years later, a Rwandan farmer who had become a killer during a new genocide would say: "When the killings begin, one finds oneself less embarrassed

---

www.fichierpdf.fr/2010/01/28/fgwm0f5/mein20kampf.pdf

to wield a machete than to suffer the mockery and scolding of one's comrades[5]."

Regarding the following text:

Firstly, the symptoms that can be found, in various combinations, in all so-called "mental" disorders will be discussed: anxiety, depression (stress and burn-out being their discreet veil) and delirium. It will also be mentioned a pathology which does not appear in any treatise although it is more and more widespread: the "value disease".

Some names will be frequently quoted. It is not surprising to find that of Freud, the adventurer of dreams. That of Spinoza, his approach to a "knowledge of the third kind" will often be invoked. The recourse to Einstein will undoubtedly appear more surprising. However, it is his revolutionary conception of space-time that resonates with the most enigmatic of Freud's questions concerning

---

5. "Group dynamics, mimetic gregariousness of individuals in a group" (N. Truong), "Will to do as the others do" (J. Sémelin). "For the Rwandan farmer, taunts are more difficult to face than blood on the machete", Jean HATZFELD *in* "De la guerre à l'idéologie, réflexions sur les ressorts de l'engrenage génocidaire", *Le Monde*, 4 April 2014, p. 18-19.

the "psychic apparatus". Finally, Eisenstein is very present because of his theory of montage which had made him discover, he said, "the formula of the pathetic". But also because of the place of music in his reflection. As early as antiquity, one speaks of "music of the spheres". Eisenstein had the strange, but unrealized, project of writing a "spherical" book one day. It was as if he wanted to recall the unspoken dimension of certain circular books, ending with the feeling of renewed energy that had been necessary to write them. The *Ethics* and *In Search of Lost Time*, for example. What invisible universe did the very editing of each of these books secretly express? That of madness perhaps, the *singularity* of Spinoza, of Proust. The way they had had to refuse the norms, the limits of their time. Before, not without anguish, daring to transgress them.

1. Anxiety

"The self is the true locus of anguish."
S. Freud, *Inhibition, Symptom and Anxiety.*

Millions of children die of hunger every year on the planet, inequalities are increasing, a barbarism is underway. We *know* all this, but we don't really *understand it. When* asked by a journalist what he had been thinking during his mission, a bomber pilot replied: "I couldn't get my mind off the hundred and seventy-five dollars I still have to pay for the refrigerator[6]. Thus there is a general denial-or displacement-of anxiety.

Rarely admitted, especially by men who believe it to be a "sign of weakness", fear is the most

____

6. Günther ANDERS, *The Obsolescence of Man*, Éditions Ivrea, Paris, 2012, p. 299.

universal and most hidden feeling. Alain Veinstein's courageous description of his own anguish has the merit of reminding us of its origin. His confession will surprise many. Many will think that he is exaggerating, that he is overdoing it, so much so that the anguish of the other is readily ignored or underestimated:

> *"Fear brings us back to childhood.* And I tell myself that in their eyes, of course, to them who confide in me their fear, the authors I interview, I must appear as the child who, unlike them, spends his nights alone without being afraid. If they only knew the torments I have always had to face. At first I was petrified with terror. Fear clutched my throat, pounded my chest, overwhelmed me in wave after wave. Sweat flooded my forehead, I could feel it dripping down my ribs, I was shaking so badly that I couldn't hold my paper.
>
> "And yet I needed it, my paper, for I was so anxious that I had to write down word for word all my questions. I clung to my index cards, even the word "Good evening" was written, and even my name, in the end *disclaimer*, because I assure you I didn't know who I was anymore. I was wrapped up in fear like a mummy in its bandages.

The use of the imperfect tense should not be misleading,
the fear did not leave me[7] [...]"

The anguish is a fear without object, one says. Without an obvious object, we should specify. What anguish hides, indeed, is a piece of badly forgotten childhood, of the past disguised as future. But to really understand it, it is necessary to reintegrate affectivity into rationality, which nobody had done before Spinoza. More than two centuries before Freud discovered the associative thought to which we will return at length.

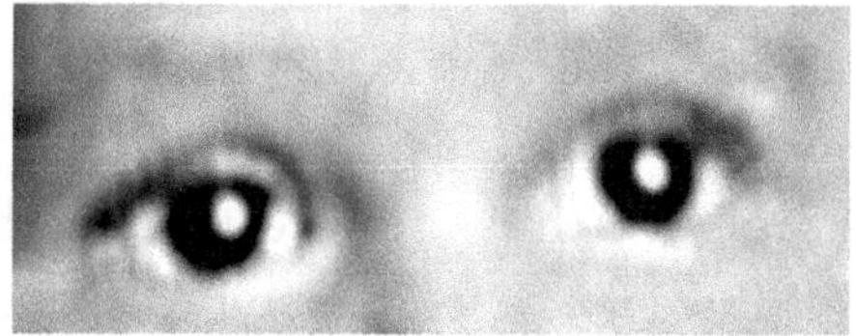

____

7. Alain Veinstein, France Culture, "*Du jour au lendemain* a vingt ans", broadcast on September 17, 2005 (my italics). To be compared with what Hélène Jouan, a journalist at France Inter, said: "When the red light comes on, I have the anguish of not being able to get a sound out" in *Télérama*, 22 June 2016.

1. Anxiety

Because the affect, infinitely faster than light, abolishes time. To feel, without having really remembered it, an event having taken place *years-affect* before - *the year-affect*, unit of measurement of the memory, as the year-light is for the cosmos -, it is not to *see* it, but to *live* it as it had perhaps never been lived before. To recreate it. A journey in the abolished time.

Thus the other, with a look that *affects* us, can kill us, and not only symbolically. There are suicides in companies. Teenagers harassed on Facebook kill themselves. This is because, behind all anguish, there is a power - if only the power of the words of a group - which imposes on us, by measuring us, a certain representation of ourselves. But the worst thing is that this representation is never more than a cliché. An agreed role which is imposed to us without our knowledge. If we *ignore* its stereotyped character, it is because it revived an old image of ourselves, until then *unconscious*, sometimes painful, which submerged us. The unrecognized and the unconscious thus occult each other.

The double secret, a painting by Magritte. Two representations of the same face. In one, a part of the face is missing, as if it had been cut out. In the other, the face is whole, but it has lost its gaze to an excavation strewn with bells (there is also a bell in Proust at the end of *Time Regained*) suggesting potentially murderous resonances.

The apparently mysterious essence of anguish lies in this double secret. A twisted entanglement. The fear of being rejected if we do not accept the role that a group destines to us. And, at the same time, the loss of our gaze, the unbearable narrowing of possibilities, that this submission awakens. We find here both Bourdieu - the relations of power in a certain field - and Lacan's "stage of the mirror": the assignment to a child of a "me" by the look, by the words of the other.

A certain representation of ourselves is thus the point of support *of* an *ontological lever* that more or less voluntarily all the powers use. A lever that allows them, like Archimedes, to raise a world, the invisible world of our memory, to arrange it without our knowledge, and to project it disguised as the future. How to make understand to who is in the deceptive certainty of the anguish that we can, by spotting the double bottom, unmask the false evidence and make it move back?

Because anguish has nothing "metaphysical" about it. It is banal, common, daily. Like the one that, at the beginning of the school year, knots the stomachs of the students. But also - what these pupils ignore - the belly of their teachers. And we must never forget the anguishing lack of money, which, curiously, is never mentioned. "When you talk to someone about money, their face changes, and what do you see? Anxiety. I've noticed it a hundred times. It's as if you're touching the very sources of life[8]."

Fear, so often ignored, is indeed a major political issue. Fear changes sides during certain events, the Popular Front for example, or May 68. Or more banally during a strike. It is this oblivion that makes any servitude enigmatic, never in reality "voluntary", contrary to what La Boétie said. What can indeed remain of "will" in a being who has lost his look because a power has strangled his desire by depressing him - sometimes to the point of suicide?

It is therefore essential to learn not to fear one's own anguish. It attests to the strength to exist. A fight. It is even a line of defense against the desperate stasis of depression. This is what must be transmitted. Who will write *Anguish, instructions for use*? To say that

---

8. Julien GREEN, *Diary (1956-1972)*, November 10, 1967, in *Œuvres complètes,* t. V, "Bibliothèque de la Pléiade", Gallimard, Paris, 1977, p. 443.

beings, contrary to grains of filings, can *get out of it* if they manage to represent the lines of force of the field where they are caught. A "pedagogy of anguish", it is undoubtedly what one should register very early in the school programs.

This universal fear, faced with the threat that *the other* represents, no one has described it better than Hegel. He speaks of it as a "primordial fear, an absolute fear that makes a consciousness stagger[9]". A "necessary" fear, he insists, because it alone attests that with this other, there is a *real relation*.

The anguish in front of the other, that Hegel describes, is the conscience of a mortal risk indeed, we have seen it. The one of a diminishment of oneself, apparently irremediable if the other manages to impose to our conscience a certain image of ourselves. To insult, or even simply to make a value judgment, is to try to make the other fall into a desperate assembly of his memory. "You're not smart." Such words can induce a feeling of exclusion *and at the same time* a real reorganization, a reductive *editing* of the whole

---

9. G.W.F. HEGEL, "The struggle of the opposite self-consciousnesses", in *The Phenomenology of Spirit*, t. I, Aubier, Paris, 1980, p. 158-166.

1. Anxiety

memory, a sorting out retaining from the film of our past only the scenes where we "did not measure up", confirming to us that indeed "we are not intelligent[10]". *Old roles* then strangle us the melody. It is thus not astonishing that to Freud and his patients, taken in the mythology of the masculine/feminine reigning at the time, this sensation of *reduction* of the being - consequence of a montage - evokes a "castration".

We will come back to this concept of "assembly" at length.

To listen to an anguished being, thus, is to be *attentive to his style* rather than to his manners. To hear his rhythms, to know how to support his dissonances. Musical counter-field. This very attention, this movement of recognition of a singularity must have the mobility, the imagination, the creative freedom of a dream. This slightly crazy generosity which deconstructs all the montages: it happens that an anguish disappears when, in a relation not excluding the humor, the social roles simply fade away. There is no longer, for example, a doctor and a patient, but two beings a little uncomfortable face to face. If, as the

---

10. Nathalie SARRAUTE describes this beautifully in *disent les imbéciles,* "Blanche", Gallimard, Paris, 1976, p. 41-50.

meeting progresses, the doctor has gradually relaxed and taken the risk of fully listening to him, he then offers his patient the spectacle, the demonstration, that a cure is possible. Listening attentively to the resonances, but welcoming the unexpected, can indeed be surprisingly liberating. Allowing the other to rebuild himself. Silently then - one could hear an unknown note flying -, two beings find themselves, sometimes love each other, allied in a fight that is common to them. The one which has for end to assume, each one - let us dare the neologism -, its *dingularity*. The only way to persevere in one's being. Spinoza here anticipates Freud.

Anguish and "death drive"? Satan is not necessary

"A thing can only be destroyed by an external cause."

"Everything, as far as it can, strives to persevere in its being."

"The effort (*conatus*) by which each thing strives to persevere in its being is nothing outside the actual essence of that thing."

Baruch Spinoza, *Ethics*, III, 4, 6, 7.

Freud should be read as Spinoza read Descartes. With attention - even tenderness at times, he was so alone at the beginning - but with a critical eye. The gaze that he himself never lost with regard to his own text of 1920, *Beyond the Pleasure Principle*, where, coming out of the war and having just lost his daughter, he hypothesizes a "death drive (*Todestrieb*)". "I am not convinced myself," he said of this essay, which was more speculative than clinical, unlike all his previous works. And in view of the success of this work, a success that surprised him, he even wrote with his usual humor: "It's very popular and has earned me a lot of letters and praise. I must have made a big mistake there[11]. Nevertheless, until the end of his life, he will maintain his hypothesis. This hypothesis was curiously supported in large part (not less than half of the text) by biological data (embryology, reproduction of unicellular and multicellular organisms), a kind of argument that he had not been used to until then. This death drive opposed to the life drive, Thanatos against Eros, Freud brings it

---

11. "Letter to Eitingon," March 27, 1921, *in* Peter GAY, *Freud, a life*, Hachette, Paris, 1991, p. 463, reissued by Fayard, Paris, 2013.

closer to the repetition compulsion, its "demonic" character, before writing curiously: "I have played the devil's advocate." To which Primo Levi, speaking of Auschwitz, seems to reply: "It has been said, and it is an obscenity, that the world needs conflict: that the human race cannot do without it. These are captious and suspect arguments. Satan is not necessary[12]..." And, speaking of the SS guards: "With one exception, they were not monsters, they had our faces, but they had been poorly educated [...] subordinates [...] fearing punishment [...] too obedient[13] [...]"

The stake of the debate is capital. If "one is born violent", indeed, if the cause of anguish resides in a kind of fundamental aggressiveness, one can have fought victoriously a power source of oppressions and inequalities, there will always remain "in" the man a propensity to destroy himself and the other. There is thus something desperate - dangerous perhaps: "the axis of evil" - in what is presented to us as an "inner" necessity. And here we see the "inside"/"outside" division appearing, as if the "inside" were something

______

12. Primo LEVI, *Les naufragés et les rescapés. Forty years after Auschwitz*, "Arcades", Gallimard, Paris, 1989, p. 197.
13. *Id. at* 199.

1. Anxiety

other than the badly forgotten past. A history from which we have never recovered, that of our encounter with the other, the mode according to which it has one day *affected* us. The *look of the other* marks the entry in *the symbolic order*, an anguish to which we will be confronted all our life. The history of these affects, beyond good and evil, can be found in Book III of the *Ethics*. Spinoza announces there, three hundred years before, the Freud of 1900, the one of *The Interpretation of Dreams* and Free Association[14]. The man who had proposed a certain way of *listening to* the other.

Now I remember. A nurse is climbing over the railing on the seventh floor of the hospital where I work. We catch her. Death wish? No. A word she had been called. Just a word. The only one, no doubt, that could kill her.

---

14. *Ethics*, III, 13, 14, 15, 16, with their demonstrations, corollaries, scholias. We read in particular: "Love is nothing else (*nihil aliud*) than joy accompanied by an external cause; and hate, nothing else than sadness accompanied by the idea of an external cause." But also: "From the mere fact that an object has something similar to another object which usually affects the mind with joy or sadness; and although that by which this object resembles the previous one is not the efficient cause of this affect, we will have for it, however, love or hate."

Lessons of solitude

Hospital.

There are few places where anguished solitudes are so dramatically brought together. Patients' anxiety, of course. But also that of the caregivers. A meeting of faces, bodies, movements, rhythms.

Fugacious: the elevator.

There is more in a hospital elevator than in all of philosophy. All of them, one against the other. The glances: antennae, tentacles, pseudopods that seek each other, brush against each other, feel each other. Lingering, evading. Warm or icy. How are you? You have to be. Like a Monday. Doctors and nurses. Men and women, white and black. Brief encounters. Students, course handouts in hand. Interns coming off shift, relieved, wacky, cool, deceptively casual. Teachers and hall boys. Close by, touching each other. Ignoring each other. Brief glance at the badge. Naked symbolism. Imperceptible, present, painful borders. To be or not to be. Who is it? Oh yes. First names, first names. Hello! A patient lying on a stretcher seems lost. Reassure him. A few words. And don't forget to buy a newspaper because at the consultation you will have to wait. How long will it take? I don't know. Pediatrics, seventh floor. Charlotte. Shy, afraid. "Is this your blanket? - Yes", with a nod. Quickly teddy bear disappears. Hidden behind her back. Secret garden. Private life. Oh dear! False move. Back to the basement. The radio, the morgue.

Painful: the visit.

An unspoken, yet blinding hierarchy. White coats and pyjamas. The medical language. 'It's a toxo. He's in low flow." "What are they saying? I can't hear." TV in every room. Living, suffering, raving, dying in front of the small screen. What's wrong with him? What do we do? Oxygen. The pain woke her up last night. Morphine doesn't work anymore. She's suffocating. I hope I didn't screw up. I have to ask the boss, the chief, anyone, because I don't know. What the hell am I doing here? Don't panic. Protect yourself. The right distance, not too close and not too far. Be part of the team. *Publish or perish*. The *New England Journal of Medicine*. Will I get my hospital practice position? I am more clinical than Eric but he has more international publications. Doing outings. "Yes, ma'am? I told you, we don't have the results yet. But of course, as soon as we have it. No, nothing to worry about!" Exchanging glances. A quick meeting with a patient. A fleeting, essential complicity. On the quiet. In rupture with the medical group. Outlaw listening.

Torn: strike notice.

Strike decided. Difficult in a hospital. The anguish changes sides. Of tone. The revolution. As if a rhythm that was previously contained could now express itself. Would there be a struggle of rhythms? The unions. Do not let yourself be recuperated. "I don't do politics." THE GA. Debates. Public speaking. Voting. "Patients should not be used as hostages." Urgent care to be provided. One problem: the definition of "emergency"? Giving drinks, passing the bedpan: urgent. "Not enough nurses, caregivers. Not paid enough." Agreed. But still. Contagious strike. "Do you have any information?" Media. Whispered rumors. "General Intelligence is in the lobby." Negotiations. "This comes at the worst possible time. Crisis. Budget cuts." Tough stance. Hesitations. The space of the hospital has curved strangely. The usual words, gestures are as if diverted. Fear. Everyone is afraid. Could the strikes have a latent content? It is impossible to reach the director. "I heard he's going

1. Anxiety

to jump." Pay for the days of walkout. Are you dreaming or what? Strike of the guards? No way. Don't give in. Don't be manipulated. "You have to know how to end a strike." You think? Resumption. Early chilly morning. Two incoming: unexplained fever, attempted suicide. Resumption. In the caretakers, in the pit of the stomach, a strange feeling, an incomprehensible guilt. Ambivalence.

Ambivalence. Don't lose the south

"Many times I would have been happy to see him disappear from the world, but I know that if that happened I would be even more upset. In short, I don't know how to deal with this devil of a man!"

Plato, *The Banquet,* Alcibiades (216c).

From Alcibiades to little Hans, from the rat man to Marcel Proust, it is the troubling enigma of ambivalence - love/hate - that we find in stories where anguish turns into violence.

To desire the death of whom one loves. From this unacknowledged - unacknowledged because it is unbearable - is born a guilt. Hence the hatred, always masked. Sudden annoyance, incomprehensible pity, excessive solicitude: disguised witnesses of ambivalence.

It is from a rhythm that we must start. A pulse.

To go to the other without losing oneself.

To go to the other, all histories confused, in a thunderbolt. Two styles, one identification. Magic.

And then come back, find each other again, sometimes not immediately. To recreate ourselves.

What is left of our love? What remains of this symbolic score in which I am inscribed, which confronted yours for the time of a beat, the time of a tear? What has become of my staves? What remains of my tonality after this meeting of our two scores, this arm wrestling of sexes, ages, classes, this fight of cannibal groups in which you and I, since before our birth, were already inscribed? Battlefield of the History (with a big axe, as Perec said) the *symbolic* is strewn with wrecks of this struggle. Egos, always victims of a power.

Because if the imaginary - tinkering from fragments of the past (not creation *ex nihilo*) - walks to the love, joining together tirelessly the notes which like themselves and the representations which resemble themselves, the symbolic functions to the exclusion: to be in or not, of such or such clan. Process

1. Anxiety

at the same time unconscious and misunderstood. Incomprehensible.

"I don't understand." Is he silly! "It's my stupidity", said little Hans when talking about his phobia. The same words, curiously, in the mouth of Heidegger (*eine grosse Dummheit*) when he evoked retrospectively, but without analyzing it, his blindness towards Nazism. Stupidity has no existence in itself. It is a circulatory arrest, a clot of meaning.

But Sartre is right: stupidity is only a form of oppression.

Under the gaze of the other, I sometimes lose my bearings.

I am afraid.

But to lose the north in front of the other, it is to be victim of a trick of escamotage. Not to *see* any more that the glance which lit up, in front of me (left rectangle of the diagram[15]) is in reality (right rectangle) only a coproduction: an eye, and a *montage*

---

15. Scheme of course "impossible" since it claims to represent, in space, a "*circulation* in time (the right rectangle) between dimensions, of which one is partly unknown (the symbolic), the other (the memory, the imaginary) partly unconscious. This figuration aims only at doing justice to the transversal cutting (left rectangle): "outside" (the glance of the other) / "inside" (the "me").

of my memory, of my history, nothing but a projected montage, rolled up around this eye.

And it is, at the same time, to lose the south. I amalgamating a certain image of myself, of which I forget the relative nature, a function of the group of which it is only a fragment: I feel, in spite of myself, "the white man" in Africa, a role that, precisely, the editing of my memory has imposed on me.

All this I no longer perceive, because the *meridian of* reality has turned. It was until now vertical (right rectangle): memory | symbolic. It has become horizontal (left rectangle), an *equator* which, illusorily, would separate an "inside" (the "psyche") and an "outside" (the "external" world).

Clac! Back to reality (right rectangle). The illusion dissipates. What the horizontal cutting, "outside"/"inside", had stolen from the consciousness is then revealed: the "look of the other" and the "me" are deconstructed.

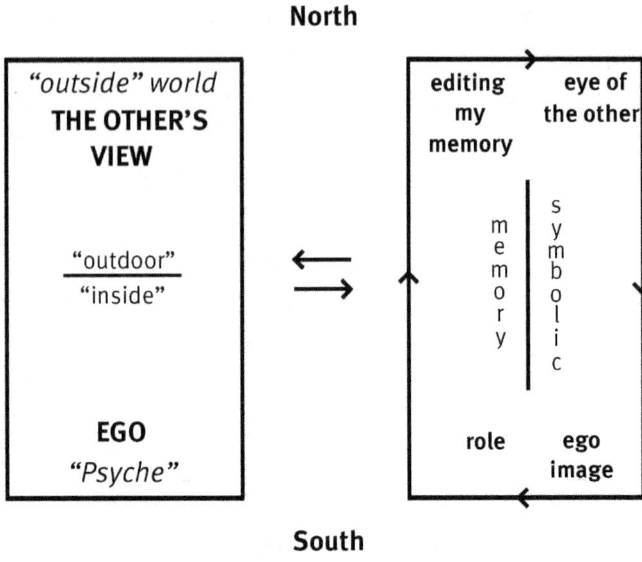

Rimbaud won! "Swept away, the millions of skeletons of the old imbeciles who had found only the false meaning of the self. "I is another." The copper can wake up clarion, "there is nothing of its fault." The brass is made to sound joyfully, without worrying about its role in the orchestra, even if it can happen to a bugler to murder a clarinet.

To feel good ("in one's skin", as we say), is to move in the right direction. The image of the self - cause of discomfort - is then unmasked, relativized before being erased. It is to this that the interpretation of a dream, sometimes, can give access.

The ambivalence cut in two by the vertical of the found time (right rectangle), the glance of the other pierced with day, the hatred is put back in its place. My desire to destroy you becomes again a reassuring nonsense. Of this *symbolic* murder, a symbolic put in its place, I am not guilty any more.

I will finally be able to love you without fear, of all my history to which its flexibility - all its possible assemblies - was returned.

Father, *I hate* you. I *hate* you, and it doesn't matter anymore.

It was the group of sons - and me inside - against the group of fathers. All these little bodies, naked like those of the Auschwitz deportees, against their torturers; the group of wild animals against the group of trainers, dogs against trainers. Hate of the training.

A son, you too have been.

They will be able to meet, our stories of sons, of wild animals, our stories of dogs.

We will finally know that neither you nor I had anything to do with it.

1. Anxiety

I will be able to hate you properly, symbolically, my love will have regained all its meaning.

We will be able to dismantle the magic tricks and the tents, leave the village of anguish, take back the caravan and leave together on the roads.

A circulation was re-established, that of the sense: the real. From now on, only it will be able to bite me. The concepts of dogs can continue to bark, they will not frighten me any more. They will not depress me any more.

In the early morning, the wind is often a bit strong.

2. Depression

"A power, quick, or I'll get depressed!" Arrival of Nounours

"Depression" is a depressing term because it seems to have no remedy. "Depression" sounds more accurate. Or depreciation. Words that evoke a loss of self-esteem. A *devaluation* that leads to a weakening of the ability to anticipate, to desire. A restriction of emotional investments. An overwhelming, permanent weariness, "from the morning", the overwhelming feeling of living (or reliving) the time of the impossible. This self-depreciation is, by far, the most frequent cause of fatigue. What exhausts, much more than any illness, is despair.

The being is an intensive concept, linked to the desire, the "force to exist", the spinozian *conatus*. The non-being, thus, is not the nothingness, it is the depression. It is thus not astonishing that it is the word of the depressed, in lack of being - "I am *worth* nothing, the life does not have any more *direction*", the theorem of the melancholy - which is able to reveal fundamental categories. The value, the sense.

Depression is the consequence of a symbolic defeat, whatever the date. A loss often seems to trigger it; in fact it reveals it.

There is a history of the impossible. Impossible which is sometimes only an old, unconscious ban. It is here that Nounours enters the scene.

> "I remember 'Teddy' being on strike."
> Béatrice Mousli in *Le Monde*, "Je me souviens de Mai 68", 6 May 2008.

Winnicott introduces us to Teddy Bear, "the transitional object". Teddy bear, small ancestor of all the prostheses, calming the anguish, consoling of the separation. "I am the gentleman who accompanies Nounours", the child seems to say, in the same tone as the president of the United States arriving in France: "I am the gentleman who accompanies Jackie Kennedy. Magic! Nounours institutes me, because of my size, transitional *subject* between my parents and him. It confers me a place in my family because Nounours is accepted by all. My relationship with him is recognized. I am no longer the child not very wise, not very clean sometimes, the sensitive note of the key of *C* major[16]. Thanks to Nounours, to remain in the musical metaphor, I now play in *B* major; my sensitive note has become the tonic. In this new hierarchy, of course, I am stuck between Mom and Teddy, but I can now integrate into the family group with an honorable status. Something like a sub-officer.

Especially since I am never separated from Teddy! To have or not to have Teddy is to be or not to be a certain child. Teddy bear, small mirror of the mother. Through you I cling to the still time of omnipotence, to the certainty of being loved, these years that I look at now through a nostalgic haze.

---

16. The sensitive note, in *C* major, is *B*. A note *in waiting*, she is gifted with a particular attraction for *C*, from which she is separated by only a semitone. "This semitone is for her a suffering. She absolutely wants to absorb it, and all classical music is saturated with this nostalgia." Henri BARRAUD, *Pour comprendre les musiques d'aujourd'hui*, Éditions du Seuil, Paris, 1968, p. 57-58.

2. Depression

"Quick, my cigarettes! My Porsche! My money! My teddy bear! My Legion of Honor!"

Proust. For a long time, his social situation had been necessary for him to survive. One day, it was no longer enough. He decides to create. It is in the apparently insignificant - but totally singular - that he finds his salvation. Madeleines, a small yellow wall, words from a dream, a small musical phrase are thus the real transitional objects - between present and past -, a way to find, by associating, a little time - in fact *meaning* - in its pure state. And *change your mood.*

He is not safe for all that. At any moment, he knows it well, according to the whims of a being, he could be again invaded by the most overwhelming sadness. As was one day one of his characters, Swann, in search of a lost melody: Odette.

And Proust describes with clinical precision the way an affect can surreptitiously infiltrate the music of a word.

A melancholic at the concert

Odette has gradually become indifferent, distracted, irritable. Swann suffers from this.

"You should go out, see people," one says to the great sorrowful. With his soul in pain, his tonal melody strewn with sensitive notes in search of a resolution, Charles Swann wanders into Mme de Saint-Euverte's salon. Mme de Guermantes is looking for him. She converses with him for a few moments. But Swann is in a hurry to get home. He so much hopes to find a word from Odette[17].

> "Swann wanted to leave, but just as he was about to escape at last, General de Froberville asked him to know Madame de Cambremer, and he was obliged to return with him to the salon to look for her.
>
> - Say, Swann, I'd rather be the husband of that woman than be massacred by the savages, what do you say?
>
> These words "massacred by savages" pierced Swann's heart painfully; immediately he felt the need to continue the conversation with the general:
>
> - Ah!" he said, "there have been beautiful lives that have ended this way... So you know... that sailor whose ashes Dumont d'Urville brought back, La Pérouse... (and Swann

---

17. Marcel PROUST, *Du côté de chez Swann. À la recherche du temps perdu*, t. I, "Bibliothèque de la Pléiade", Gallimard, Paris, new edition 1987, reprint 1991, p. 337-339.

2. Depression

was already happy as if he had been talking about Odette). It's a beautiful character and one that interests me a lot, that of La Pérouse," he added with a melancholic air.

- Ah! perfectly, La Pérouse," said the general. It is a well-known name. He has his street.

- Do you know anyone on Rue La Pérouse?" asked Swann, looking agitated.

- I only know Mme de Chanlivault, the sister of this brave Chaussepierre. She gave us a lovely evening of comedy the other day. It's a salon that will be very elegant one day, you'll see!

- Ah! she lives on rue La Pérouse. It's nice. It's a pretty street, so sad.

- But no, it's because you haven't been there for some time; it's no longer sad, it's beginning to build up, this whole neighborhood. [...] But the concert started again [...] But suddenly it was as if she had entered [...] "It's the little phrase from the Vinteuil sonata, let's not listen!"

FIRST MOVEMENT

Froberville approaches Swann. Two themes will then confront each other. Charles' desperate love, which hides behind a worldly façade. Froberville's nascent desire for the young Mme de Cambremer.

The polyphonic sentence of Froberville is simple, different melodies blending in particularly well: tone of the desiring child and conversation "between men" harmonizing with the military mode (it is general). Froberville must however modulate a little: *J'aimerais mieux être le mari* civilizes the classic "j'aimerais mieux l'avoir dans mon lit"; while *massacré par les sauvages* replaces the too noisy "boulet de canon", which one felt coming.

As banal as it is, this symbolic polyphony will nevertheless leave feathers behind as it passes through the filter of Swann's score. Froberville's request (to be presented to Mme de Cambremer) will not be heard because this score is in flames. If the words *massacred by the savages*, on the other hand, "pierce Swann's heart so painfully", it is because they resonate with the wound of his tone.

Solve this sensitive note as quickly as possible. Only Odette could do it. Let her appear! The tonic that he cannot find in his key, Swann will look for it in his modal song, devoid of a sensitive note. La Pérouse is the note he needs. It is doubly inscribed: in his tonality, it is a street where he has often been, the one where Odette lives; in his modal song, in principle less dangerous, La Pérouse is a sailor massacred by savages. But Swann's

2. Depression

tonal song, which he tries to repress, is still there, though reduced to its simplest expression, an affect: *sad and pretty*. It is this affect, still a little veiled in aestheticism, that will reinvest the modal voice. From this doubly inscribed *La Pérouse*, he will structure gently, organize metaphorically the modal melody. It is *a beautiful character, and one that interests me greatly, that of La Pérouse*: Swann's sudden interest in the famous navigator is visibly tinged with a certain melancholy.

It is in a neutral register, the mode he has in common with Swann, their neighborhood, that of the aristocracy and the upper middle class, that Froberville will hear Swann's melody: *Ah! perfectly, La Pérouse, says the general. It is a well-known name. He has his street.*

If Swann looks agitated when he asks: *"Do you know anyone on Rue La Pérouse?" it is because* the chord Froberville has just struck makes him fear an attempt to modulate his own tone, the private garden where he is secretly playing with Odette's image.

I only know Mme de Chanlivault," said Froberville, who, having noticed Swann's bad appearance, his sudden trouble, and knowing his relations with Odette, now understood, at last, that he had to be reassured. He therefore reverts to the modal, worldly melody, by which he knows he can, with the least risk, communicate with Swann; Mme de Chanlivault then arrives at the right moment to urgently neutralize Odette whose dangerous presence he has just suspected.

La Pérouse versus *massacred by savages, Chanlivault* versus *Odette*: a kind of counterpoint. However, the evocation of the young socialite, *who will one day have a very elegant salon, you'll see!* indicates that Froberville's modal melody is also emotionally impregnated with its insistent tonal theme: "a young woman full of hopes".

But Swann does not hear it that way, he manages to slip his theme back in: *a pretty street, so sad*. Two themes, one following the other like its shadow. A double fugue.

It is no longer sad, it is beginning to be built, all this district. Froberville has, one last time, placed his motif, always the same: the color of his budding desire for Mme de Cambremer. A door knob would have been considered full of promise by Froberville at that moment, and of dark beauty by Swann.

SECOND MOVEMENT

The concert resumed. The little phrase of the Vinteuil sonata then melts on Swann. He is again

2. Depression

painfully pierced, but this time without remedy, as if the music, suddenly erasing the words, had swept away all his defenses. "Delivered by the sound of the object, here is consciousness in the presence of its pure powers and its most intimate laws. And music will only be the incarnation of this self-consciousness that thought acquires by means of sounds[18]. It is precisely these hidden movements, their subtle harmony, these fluctuations, that music mimes and reveals. Certain melancholic people, thus, have horror of it, tonal music which plays the succession of tensions and resolutions, of suffering and cheerfulness, these fights of which they became incapable; modal music, often so close to a depressive experience, with its strange modes, exotic or medieval, which are recognized with their only harmony, as a foreign language means to us immediately its country of origin. A lost paradise, perhaps, that of a child's sleigh, for example, in *Citizen Kane*. Music where we sometimes feel (notably in certain pieces of Satie) that there has been a separation, that the loss is final. And that madness is undoubtedly not far away.

18. Gisèle Brelet, *Le temps musical. Essai d'une esthétique nouvelle de la musique* (1949), PUF, Paris, 1953.

3. The delirium

Delusion, reality, truth

The delirious word anguishes because, one feels it immediately, no negotiation will be possible. *Untameable* otherness, it evades understanding. Enigma, it challenges all theories.

"What has been foreclosed, rejected from the symbolic, reappears in the real", formulated in his own vocabulary, is the process imagined by Lacan to explain the mechanism of delirium. This hypothesis has the interest of proposing a certain model. The reappearance in one point of what has disappeared in another point, this is indeed how the existence of a *circulation* is demonstrated.

The *real* would then be something like the setting in motion of a *reality*. Reality that should not be confused with *truth*, that regional specialty. The real - a term of logic (true/false) - is only a piece of reality, a territory enclosed within hedges, often "linguistic", set up by a community. *Here, I am happy*, said a German Jew who emigrated to the United States, *aber glücklich bin ich nicht.* Two languages. Two apparently contradictory truths. One reality.

A patient, Mr. A***, presents himself under a false name, a false address. A profession that he has never practiced. His behavior is otherwise quite "normal". Mythomaniac? Not so simple. We soon learn that he was hospitalized in a neighboring country for delusions: he thought he was an international spy. A spy, in order to hide his activity, to pass unnoticed, must constantly lie. At this price, Mr. A*** was, apparently, in the real world. One day, he decided to tell the truth, *his truth,* and "confessed" to us that he was the agent of a foreign power. He was then finally clearly, in our eyes, in a delirium. That day, he drank his urine.

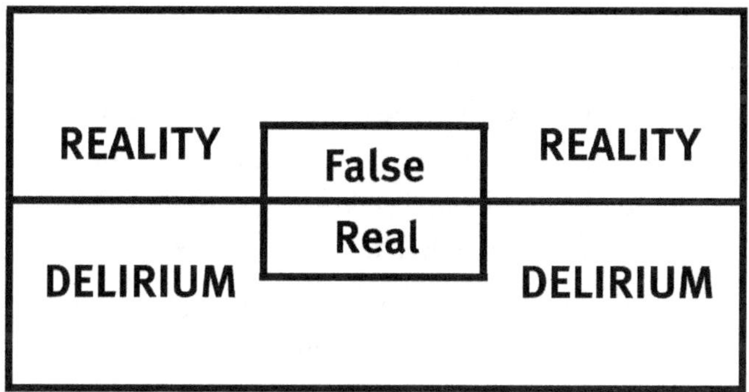

True or false. A hallucination, a delirium, are given for the truth. An unshakeable conviction: a *belief*. Let us specify that it will be here above all question of delirium of the paranoid type. The certainty that accompanies this delirium signs its origin: the *symbolic*. Its logic cut with a knife where the eye of the other - an eye is there, often, in the pictures painted by psychotics - and a latent violence are always present. Nothing comes to nuance the peremptory of this crazy logic. No analogical blur, not even the slip of a metaphor.

A word becomes *delirious* when it *short-circuits* the memory, so to speak. The adaptive flexibility of the memory, of its potential assemblies, certainly, does not go without risks. Anxiety, depression, as we have seen, painfully attest to this - but without breaking with reality. The delirious discourse, on the other hand, goes all stiff, straight in its boots, from the south to the north[19], making directly, in a senseless way, the representation. For what it projects there are words, images, devoid of *meaning* but not of significance, in this or that code, since, cut off from memory, they come exclusively from the symbolic[20].

On a musical score, one could imagine something like a drama in harmony. The notes of a modal melody, suddenly unable to merge, in a chord, with those of a tonal line. What distinguishes talent from madness, Freud from Schreber, Lacan's writing from that of Aimée, his psychotic patient[21], is the degree of *negotiation* to which they have each reached between their own melodic lines. Perhaps, in order not to sink

---

19. See right-hand rectangle in diagram on p. 36.
20. A symbolic anemic, deprived of the *sense* that a circulation passing by the memory, the bank of the sense, brought to him. Memory "perforated" because, undoubtedly, *something*, one day, could not find a place there. Its place. Something *unassimilable*.
21. Jacques LACAN, *De la psychose paranoïaque dans ses rapports avec la personnalité*, "Points Essais," Éditions du Seuil, Paris, 1980, reprinted Points, Paris, 2015. This is Lacan's doctoral thesis in medicine.

into madness, it is necessary to learn to move with flexibility, agility between these different melodic lines, even if it means, like Bartok, reinventing *an elusive tonality*, in order to remain able to modulate, to adapt to reality.

During a delirium, on the contrary, only remain, projected, the logical assemblies of the *symbolic*, rigid devices, based on codes of groups - family, social -, with their regulations, their laws. Nothing surprising if the walls look, if they speak, if the delirious speeches are invaded by the projection of political or advertising stereotypes, of clichés[22]: a certain interpretative logic using pieces of the symbolic speech. "To be or not to be; friend or enemy".

The entry into delirium can be triggered - there is only a symbolic threshold - by any event, a promotion for example.

Schreber was appointed president of the chamber of the Dresden court of appeal and took up his post

---

22. "T'es pas un homme!", "Tu es moche !", "Tu es bête !", "Personne ne t'aime", ricanaient les voix" *in* "Mauvaises voix", *Le Monde*, July 6, 2003, by Florence Beaugé who quotes Polo Tonka, *Dialogue avec moi-même. Un schizophrène témoigne*, presented and commented by Philippe Jeammet, Odile Jacob, Paris, 2013.

3. The delirium

on October 1st, 1893. He fell ill at the end of that month[23]. The switch is the appearance of a signifier - a title, a date - unassimilable by memory. An image of the unbearable self, unbearable. He lived in *C* major. One day an *alteration* occurs. One of his notes became foreign to him.

Several possibilities, then:

1° Act as if nothing had happened, "don't know it", continue in *C* major with a weight on your stomach. Invading all perception, this painful foreign body will grow in size as if it were a monster or a cancer. The patient, who has become a president and hypochondriac, will then run to doctors who will palpate his abdomen for a long time, in vain. He will consult other doctors. Sometimes he will give birth to a book. Or, like Freud, of a theory: "The future will tell if the theory contains more madness than I would like, or the madness more truth than others are prepared to believe today[24]". Lacan, one evening, on television: "I cogitate madly!"

---

23. Sigmund FREUD, "President Schreber" in *Five Psychoanalyses*, PUF, Paris, 1973, p. 266.
24. *Id.* at 321.

2° More rarely, this alteration turns everything upside down. It was a hitherto unattainable status that had suddenly been offered to Schreber. His appointment to a position where he would sit among men twenty years older than him. A sun that was impossible to look at without being dazzled. An "assassination of the soul", he writes. An *unassimilable* modulation. It will be the object of a foreclosure. He had already suffered from "nervous disorders" a few years earlier when he was president of a court of first instance. This time he is delirious.

To delude, thus, is to inhabit a coherent system, purely symbolic, screaming of truth but - violence of the symbolic - potentially murderous.

Anxiety, depression, such are the risks that confrontation with the norms, with the established order, brings. The delirious reaction, on the other hand, poses a more disconcerting problem. Pascal had felt it well, who wrote: "The men are so necessarily mad, that it would be to be mad by another turn of madness, not to be mad." A statement that suggests a question: what is being crazy? Can we, for example, qualify as "objective madness", as "social psychosis" a collective aberration so universally admitted that it passes for normality: the illness of value?

4. The disease of value

There is not only the unconscious, there is also the unknown.

A communicable disease: value

"Learn to sell yourself in thirty seconds. Time yourself, film yourself, practice."

Vivian Giang, *Journal du Net. Management.*

"Can't you see that I'm burning?"

Sigmund Freud, *The Interpretation of Dreams,*

"Dream of the dead child that burns".

Workplace Suicides[25]. Self-immolation by fire. Profitability, competitiveness. Individual evaluations.

---

25. At France Telecom, an important series of suicides was recorded between 2006 and 2011. The Cachan School of Management, specially created in 2005, was entirely dedicated to the "deflation" and forced departures project. The remuneration of managers was indexed on the departures. "Getting people to

Job cuts. Not all of them died, but all of them were hit. No disease has been so long ignored. No medical treatise or psychiatric textbook has ever mentioned it[26].

It is indeed presented as a form of the "normality", the one recommended to us by the reigning ideology relayed by the big media. Additional difficulty: this pathology challenges the academic compartmentalization (sociology, psychology...). Everything happens as if, to make the diagnosis and to fight it effectively, it was necessary to pass by a new dimension - still to discover.

The disease of the market value, the exchange value, this so contagious affection, is due to a kind of virus which attacks the being in its core. To counteract its effects or even just to talk about it, the greatest caution is required. All the more so as this plague is

---

move by putting pressure everywhere... Everything was good to make the staff crack...", see Émeline CAZI, "Suicides at France Telecom: the trial is getting closer", *Le Monde,* "Supplément Éco & Entreprise", 8 July 2016, p. 3.

26. "The dignity of caregivers is violated in the name of *efficiency*. Five nurses have taken their own lives in recent months. Their distress is indicative of the managerial order that is rampant in *the hospital.* The technocratic logic must no longer overshadow the commitment of health professionals," Emmanuel HIRSCH in *Le Monde*, September 13, 2016.

accompanied by such a powerful collective denial that one must be careful not to be considered oneself as crazy, in the face of a madness from which each one believes himself spared.

In a chapter of *Capital*, as strange as the appearance of a chemical formula in Freud's inaugural dream, Marx paints a striking clinical picture of this impressive condition. It is a table that is affected. As soon as the virus has infected it, and it has thus become a commodity, "it stands up on its wooden head" and starts dancing, while contorting itself in front of the other commodities, as if it were trying to seduce them[27]. The possibility of transmission to humans is the danger of this mad table disease. Mimetons, a kind of ideological prions coming from these crazy objects, can indeed spread to almost the entire population[28]. They then turn men and women, sick without knowing it, into simple merchandise capable, by mimetic madness, in a kind of blindness

27. Karl MARX, "The fetish character of the commodity and its secret" in *Œuvres,* t. I: Économie, "Bibliothèque de la Pléiade", Gallimard, Paris, 1963, p. 604 and following.
28. Max DORRA, *Dream Struggle and Class Interpretation. Dismantling a trick of illusion,* "penser/rêver," Éditions de l'Olivier, Paris, 2013, p. 145.

(one of the signs of the disease), of spontaneously going to the market to wriggle there in turn[29]. Everything being classified, therefore classifying, they become objects of exchange, and thus play the game that is expected of them, that of "free and undistorted competition". The spectacle is indescribable, and always disturbing, in this universe where violence is never far away. All the more so as some of these human-commodities, believing that they have more "value" than the others, take advantage of this to dominate and exploit them with impunity. We are most often dealing with associations of patients grouped around a leader - generally the most affected.

Desire itself, in the world of market value, is deviated, reduced, by a kind of addiction, to looking for substitutes. Anything as long as it has the stamp, the "hierarchical claw" of a prestigious group because it is dominant.

And then there is inflation. Words and the image that humans form of themselves *during exchanges* are a kind of unpaid money: what is common between the "language" of a group and the experience, the

---

29. Pierre BOURDIEU, "Parts de marché et concurrence" in *Sur la télévision*, Liber éditions, Montréal (Québec), 1996, p. 45.

singularity of a being? It is this essential gap between form and content that explains *symbolic inflation*: there is, for example, a "wear and tear" of words. Hence the need to push the labels, to anticipate in order not to fall behind on a devaluation that we sense is inexorable. This explains the *desire for surplus value* and the strategies of bluffing, which are practically always present[30].

Thus *the self*, this crossroads, when it is reached by the disease of the value, becomes itself a value of exchange. "In a certain respect, it is of the man as of the goods. As he does not come into the world with a mirror, nor as a philosopher like Fichte, whose self needs nothing to affirm itself, he first mirrors and recognizes himself in another man[31]. This value of

---

30. "You should not try to say elegant things, designed to make you look good and to increase the esteem that people may already have for you. In other words, the only reproach I would have for you, if I may say so, is that you all want to appear too intelligent. Everyone knows you are. So why do you want to appear so?", Jacques LACAN, "The Symbolic Universe" in *The Seminar, Book II. The self in Freud's theory and in the technique of psychoanalysis,* Éditions du Seuil, Paris, 1978, p. 39.
31. Karl MARX, *Œuvres,* t. I : Économie, "Bibliothèque de la Pléiade", Gallimard, Paris, 1963, p. 582, note *a*. With this mirror, the notion of self-representation appears in *Capital.*

4. The disease of value

exchange ("to know how to sell oneself"), bound to the *evaluating glance of* the others, *means* to the self a role in which more or less *sense* will manage, as well as not, to sink.

Hence the importance of preventive action. To learn, very early, to think differently. *To turn the gaze* that enslaves you by hurting you. To resist to a scientist ideology (nothing to do with true scientificity) fetishizing the number, objectifying the beings, suppressing the affect, forbidding the dream. A world devoid of meaning. For Proust, a madeleine, one day, revealed itself to have a *meaning*. Surprising. *Invaluable.* Source of joy, the joy of having found himself by finding a lost sense, in which he will draw from now on his force of existence, the *conatus* of Spinoza.

Why speak of "disease", of "virus", about value? It is because a virus reproduces itself by parasitizing the nucleus of a cell and by grafting its own code onto it. The value, in the same way, introduces in the heart of a being - without his knowledge - a foreign *meaning*, infantilizing, misleading because it gives itself for a *meaning*. All the more so as the venal value and the

---

Note that Guy Debord, in *The Society of the Spectacle* (1967), quotes Marx about thirty times.

ANGUISH

myth of the "virile force", the symbolic violence that induces the male domination, are always entangled. "To have some or not".

In a world where words become viruses, some sentences can *kill*. Going *straight to childhood*, words impose their law. Affected, we feel "null", "guilty", "excluded". We think *we are* and we have been *fooled*. A trick of illusion at the same time ontological *and* political. Because all the memory, we will see it, is the object of a kind of assembly.

The expression "of modest origin" says it all. "Modest", the word, modestly substituted for "poor", suggests the unconscious acceptance, the internalization of the objective, statistical "bad luck" to which their social origin condemns so many beings. It insidiously incites them to moderate their aspirations. To be "reasonable"...

It is thus hardly surprising that, under a mask or another, when the most insolent social inequalities are perpetuated and *reproduced*, a depression can strike humans stigmatized by a value judgment. This depression can be due to the collapse of a self, of its image, of its rating, the origin of the crash being often multiple: suffering at work, but also unemployment, discrimination whatever it is, linked to ethnicity for

4. The disease of value

example or to age[32]. Is there - horror! - a market of desire? When he comes to believe that he will no longer arouse desire, that "beyond a certain limit his ticket is no longer *valid*", that the source of his power to exist is henceforth inaccessible to him, a being can come to eliminate himself. A murder disguised as a suicide, a "soul murder" in a room that an individual imagined to be definitively closed.

The disease of value does not need to pass through walls to kill.

The treatment of the disease of value has yet to be discovered. The elements of its diagnosis, however, have been described for nearly one hundred and fifty years by a doctor... in philosophy.

Dr. Marx: a very disturbing diagnosis

"The third great result of the emancipation of the communes is the class struggle, a struggle that fills modern history. Modern Europe was born of the struggle of the various classes of society."

---

32. "I think that in order to live, you have to start very young, because afterwards *you lose all your value* and no one will give you gifts" said Momo, the little hero of *La Vie devant soi*, by Emile Ajar, alias Romain Gary, who will commit suicide.

François Guizot, *History of Civilization in Europe*, seventh lesson, 1830.

"There is a class war, that's a fact, but it's my class, the wealthy class that is fighting it and we are winning it."
Warren Buffett, CNN interview, May 25, 2006, quoted in The *New York Times*, November 26, 2006.

Marx is probably the only philosopher to have seen three of his children die of hunger. This happened in the middle of the 19th century, in London, where he lived as an outlaw. It is noteworthy that it was *not a philosophical approach* that revealed to him the importance of economics, but his work as a journalist for the *Rheinische Zeitung* and then the *New York Tribune*. He thus discovered what was at stake in a class struggle, the *mechanism of exploitation*: if we admit that value represents human labor, surplus value is unpaid surplus labor, extorted by the dominant[33]. The last straw is that *we* then *lend to those we*

---

33. Einstein, yes Einstein, explains the mechanism of surplus value perfectly. "Insofar as the labor contract is 'free', the worker's payment takes into account his minimum needs and is calculated on the number of individuals competing for the mass of labor power needed by the capitalist, and not on the

4. The disease of value

have robbed (B. Friot), *a way of making them feel guilty by putting them in debt.* And that invariably, from generation to generation, inequalities *are reproduced.* Inequality of chances, from birth, according to social origin. A rigged game.

After a long period of blacklisting, the spectre of Marx has been making a comeback in recent years. It can be found in some books, whose signatory's name may surprise[34]. And even in magazines[35]. "A method

---

material value of the goods produced by the worker. This is the essential point: the worker's payment is not, even in principle, determined by the value of the goods he produces", Albert EINSTEIN, "Pourquoi le socialisme?" in *Œuvres choisies*, t. V, Éditions du Seuil/CNRS, Paris, 1992, p. 184.

34. Jacques ATTALI, *Karl Marx or the spirit of the world.* Fayard, Paris, 2005, p. 14-15: "Marx fascinated me by the precision of his thought, the strength of his dialectic, the power of his reasoning, the clarity of his analyses, the ferocity of his criticisms, the humor of his features, the clarity of his concepts."

35. "Marx, une analyse toujours actuelle", *Challenges*, n° 103, December 6-12, 2007; "Marx, le retour", *Courrier international,* n° 924, July 17, 2008; "Marx. Les raisons d'une renaissance", *Le Magazine littéraire,* n° 479, October 2008; "Le grand retour de Marx", *Le Nouvel Observateur,* n° 2337, August 20, 2009; "Chroniques marxiennes", France Culture, émission *Les Nouveaux Chemins de la connaissance,* from February 14 to 18, 2011; "Marx, le retour", *Philosophie Magazine,* n° 62, August 2012.

of analysis worthy of admiration", an author not very suspicious of unbridled leftism once described it[36]. "No future without Marx" wrote Derrida[37]. *The greatness of Marx* was the title of the book that Deleuze had in mind[38].

With regard to the relevance, still relevant, of Marxian analyses of economic "liberalism" - "the free fox in the free henhouse" - it is not useless to compare two discourses competing in hypocrisy to justify child labor. One is from 1866, the other from 1995 in the midst of "globalization". And it has not gotten any better[39].

---

36. Valéry GISCARD D'ESTAING, *Démocratie française*, Fayard, Paris, 1976, p. 53; and, on page 42, the concept of work-value is used...

37. Jacques DERRIDA, *Spectres de Marx*, Galilée, Paris, 1993.

38. Jean-Clet MARTIN, *Constellation de la philosophie*, Éditions Kimé, Paris, 2007, p. 135.

39. - *First text*, 1866, Vivian Hussey (a mine operator): "Is not this desire [to prohibit children under 14 from working in the mines] subordinate to the greater or lesser poverty of the parents? Wouldn't it be cruel to take this resource away from the family? Do you wish to prohibit the employment of children *underground* until they are 14 years of age in all cases?" *Report from the Select Committee of Mines*, July 23, 1866 *in* Karl MARX, *Works I, Economics,* Appendix IX, "Bibliothèque de la Pléiade", Gallimard, Paris, 1963, p. 1330. - *Second text*, 1995, on child

4. The disease of value

Read Le Capital, but not only

> "Does the class struggle have a latent content?"
> Henri Lefebvre, *The Differentialist Manifesto.*

It is for having unmasked this violent and perfectly concealed cheating that Marx is hated, feared, censored, victim of a real omerta. The "Phynance pump" being, according to Jarry, coupled to the "machine to discombobulate", to say oneself "Marxist[40]" on the media, is to expose oneself to

---

labor in Bogota, New Delhi, and Marrakech, *The Economist* (April 9, 1994): "The cost of subordinating trade to human rights would outweigh the expected benefits." A professor at Cornell University in the United States suggests: "If child labor must remain illegal where it is aberrant, as in rich countries, another approach must be considered when it represents a mass phenomenon [...], it would be a disaster for many families threatened with perishing if their children were no longer allowed to work," *International Herald Tribune*, November 30, 1994, quoted by Serge HALIMI, "Enfants rois" in *Le Monde diplomatique*, January 1995, p. 13. The number of working children has decreased over the last ten years, but it was still estimated at 168 million in 2013 by the International Labour Organization (ILO), a specialized agency of the UN.

40. "Marxism is the name that in France and elsewhere has always been given to socialism when one wanted to fight it, vilify it, extirpate it. It was to Marxism that Mussolini declared war. It is Marxism that Hitler, Göring and their gang want to tear out

the qualification of "old-fashioned", of "archaic" (which is never the case when one declares oneself "platonist"!). And not to be listened to anymore. A certain number of "progressive" parties have even consigned Marx to oblivion, stupidly throwing away a scanner - a diagnostic instrument - on the pretext that it had not cured the patient[41]. They have thus allowed themselves to be deprived of a particularly enlightening interpretive grid, provided that they do not use it dogmatically, exclusively. A belief. For the emergence of a discovery allowing a better perception of reality - this is also true for Freud's discovery - always risks being treated as a religious "revelation", an article of faith.

---

of German soil. Whoever attacks socialism, whoever wants to make fun of it or make it an object of hatred, calls it Marxism. All the more reason to raise proudly, like the beggars of William of Orange, the name under which they claim to mock or accuse us. Yes we are Marxists, yes we are internationalists. We know perfectly well what this profession of faith exposes us to" (Léon Blum), *in* Jean LACOUTURE, *Léon Blum*, Éditions du Seuil, Paris, 1977, p. 238.

41. "I have never established a 'socialist system'...", Karl MARX, *Œuvres*, t. II: Économie (suite), "Bibliothèque de la Pléiade", Gallimard, Paris, 1968, p. 1532 and 1536.

4. The disease of value

The reading of Marx has often been described as a revelation, a shattering event. By Gide[42], by Beauvoir: "This notion of surplus value gave me a shock when I was 18 or 19. I really understood exploitation, injustice in a way that I only sensed[43]. By Sartre: "I came from a bourgeois background that, as a result, had not even heard of the class struggle[44]." It is indeed striking that the concept of class struggle is both unknown and misunderstood. *Unknown*, stubbornly, because of the guilt that it arouses while it reveals a logic, without referring to a moral. There is neither "good" nor "bad" here, but only beings plunged by chance into a cold logic, that of profit and a hidden power relationship. The crazy, Ubuesque logic of the world of value, fetishizing merchandise and money, which, without their knowledge, dictates the behavior of these beings. A concept moreover completely *incomprehensible* if one does not perceive its latent

---

42. André GIDE, *Journal 1889-1939*, "Bibliothèque de la Pléiade", Gallimard, Paris, 1957, p. 1280.

43. Simone DE BEAUVOIR, *La Cérémonie des adieux* followed by *Entretiens avec Jean-Paul Sartre août-septembre 1974*, Gallimard, Paris, 1981, p. 481-482.

44. Jean-Paul Sartre quoted *in* Simone DE BEAUVOIR, *La Cérémonie des adieux* followed by *Entretiens avec Jean-Paul Sartre août-septembre 1974*, *op. cit.* p. 486.

content: the experience of an injustice, of a social shame. An anguish whose translation is violence[45]. It is enough to walk through the streets of Montreuil and Neuilly to see the evidence.

The "middle class," however, the grey zone, blurs the picture, prompting further analysis. The sometimes fascistic position of some of its members can certainly be explained, in part, by the fact that they are the most threatened by globalization[46]. It remains

---

45. "To read Bourdieu in the 1970s was - and still is - to feel a violent *ontological shock*: *the being that one believed to be is no longer the same, the vision that one had of oneself and of others* in society is torn apart. And, if one comes from the dominated social strata, the intellectual agreement is doubled by the feeling of the lived evidence, of the veracity of the theory: the reality of the *symbolic violence*", extract from Annie ERNAUX, "Bourdieu: le chagrin", *Le Monde*, February 5, 2002. "The inaugural lesson at the Collège de France [...] the feeling of being perfectly unworthy [...] a feeling of guilt with regard to my father [...] Nuits d'insomnie [...] the social consecration that offends *my image of myself* [...]" *in* Pierre BOURDIEU, *Esquisse pour une auto-analyse*, Éditions Raisons d'agir, Paris, 2004, pp. 136-139.
46. "The global crisis has the effect of opposing the interests of the French non-wage-earning petty bourgeoisie and those of the internationalized French bourgeoisie, which relocates and sells in different countries, thus reducing its dependence on the French economy [...] There is therefore a real class struggle within the bourgeoisie, the petty and the large," Hélène MARCHAL and

4. The disease of value

to understand the terrifying passage, always possible, from the fear of bankruptcy to nationalist and racist ferocity. And it is here that we must invoke factors other than the economy[47]. Among these factors, the macho discourse of male domination, whose importance should not be underestimated. Aren't "virile" watchwords omnipresent - the cult of the leader, of the national warrior - in all dictatorships, including Mussolini's fascism and Nazism? As if in some way the gender struggle, by distributing roles[48], was *entangled* - "to have or not to have" - with the class struggle. But another logic, an individual one, must still be taken into account, one that is difficult to conceptualize - only Spinoza had ventured to do

---

Gérard MORDILLAT in *Mussolini's Fascism*, Éditions Demopolis, Paris, 2016, pp. 89-91.

47. "According to the materialist conception of history, the determining factor in history is, in the *last instance,* the production and reproduction of real life. Neither Marx nor I have ever affirmed anything more. If someone wants to distort this proposition to the point of saying that the economic factor is the *only* determining factor, he turns it into an empty, abstract, absurd sentence", Friedrich ENGELS, "Letter to Joseph Bloch", 21 September 1890.

48. "Fascism is not to prevent from saying, it is to oblige to say", Roland BARTHES, *Lessons*, Éditions du Seuil, Paris, 1978, p. 14.

so -, the logic of affects. In short, we must never forget the most ancient, fundamental, ontological anguish: that which has always been felt in the face of *the other*, the foreigner, the different. The struggle of the consciences of oneself evoked by Hegel, struggle to death, absolute fear. It will undoubtedly be up to individuals who have uncovered the anguish that all power conceals within themselves to invent the treatment that will deliver us, finally, from this delirium that is presented to us as the norm. The disease of the venal value.

The supreme irony of history is that this entangled causality was perfectly understood and cynically used by... Freud's nephew.

Freud's nephew invents the art of manipulation to sell

"A man who buys a car probably thinks he needs it to get around. His desire also likely stems from the fact that the car is a status symbol, proof of business success, a way to please his wife."

Edward Bernays, *Propaganda. How to manipulate opinion in a democracy.*

There had been Rameau's nephew, Wittgenstein's nephew, Lacan's nephew. All of them fictional characters. Edward Bernays, who died in 1995 at the age of 103, a real nephew of Freud, was the inventor, in the 1920s, just after the war, of the concept of "consumer" and of "brand image". Needs are limited, he said, but not desires. To sell, it is the desire of individuals that must be stimulated - or revealed - by "targeting" their unconscious or unacknowledged fantasies. This is what advertising does when it gives the most banal products a symbolic charge capable of modifying the representation that consumers have of themselves. And, by there, to exploit their anguish, to manipulate them. In 1929, at the request of G.W. Hill, president of the American Tobacco Company, Edward Bernays thus brought the American women to dare to smoke in public. He did this by linking the cigarette, a "phallic symbol", to the campaigns of the suffragettes fighting for women's liberation. Sales to this new clientele exploded[49].

---

49. Edward BERNAYS, *Propaganda. Comment manipuler l'opinion en démocratie*, La Découverte, Paris, 2007, p. 15-16. "The psychologists of Freud's school have shown that our thoughts and actions are compensatory substitutes for desires that we have had to repress", *id. in ibid.* p. 63.

By cynically using Dr. Karl, the commodity fetishist, and Uncle Sigmund, the desire theorist, Bernays was banking on a demand, the demand for what could be called a "symbolic prosthesis": what gives the illusion of *being*. He therefore coined the term "group spirit". How can we understand the attraction exerted (not only among adolescents) by claws, marks and other "signs of recognition" if we do not pay the attention it deserves to this intermediate level which holds such an important place in the palliative therapy of many anxieties: the *group*. This is also true for the political field. It is indeed always possible - history has tragically shown it - to see a clique emerge and take power, ready for all kinds of excesses. This clique, even if it did not possess the means of production of goods - *to have them* - would possess the means of production of anguished consciences in search of a hard drug: to *be part of* a group, of a dominant party. To have well analyzed, to have understood the dangers of the group or community illusion, it is to have already begun to guard against it.

Thus, the anguish of the individuals, a feeling of humiliation, are in the middle of a fight - of classes, but not only social - in order to persevere in their

4. The disease of value

being. It is indeed necessary for them to deliver themselves from the alienating image of themselves to which one day they were reduced: "a laborer", "a woman", "a Black", "an old man", "a madman"... Images of the self which are in fact only the ignored fragments of a discourse, of a *dominant* symbolic code. But the tragedy is that this image *imposes a role on them*. And it is here that the dimension of the *montage* intervenes, an essential articulation, that we will have to try to dismantle[50].

---

50. Eisenstein never ceased to give montage a dimension that was both dynamic - montage as *collision*, explosion - and calculated - montage organizes ideas and produces - on the psyche of the spectator - effects, emotions; see "Eisenstein, attraction du montage" *in* Dominique VILLAIN, *Le Montage au cinéma*, Cahiers du cinéma, Paris, 1991, p. 127.

5. Listening/dreaming.
Therapeutic track

I. Editing and memory: from Cantor to Eisenstein

Bipolar illness requires new concepts

"While I alternate between euphoria and discouragement, Walter Murch, the editor, is consistent, warm and reassuring."

Francis F. Coppola, Foreword to Walter Murch's book, *In the Blink of an Eye. Past, Present and Future of Editing.*

Eisenstein at his editing table.

"The big round one is the way I am when I'm fine. The small one is how I am now. Very small, reduced, shrunken... I cannot, for the moment, *reach the place* where I exist (I do not cross my own warm current, my own breath).

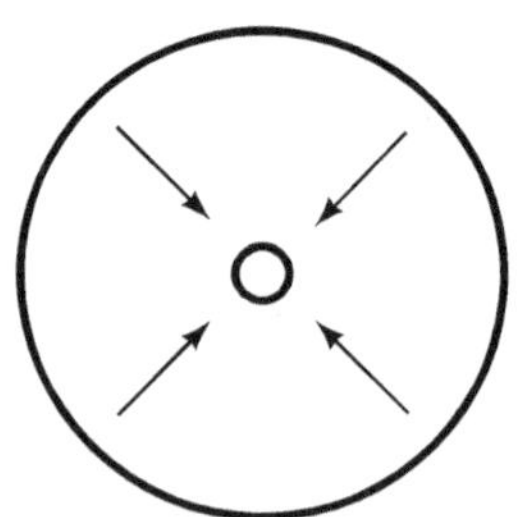

I also write to try to pierce this exteriority... I immediately come up against the walls of the very small circle in the middle of the great absent[51] [...]" Such was the image of himself that a man - a philosopher in analysis - drew, one day in January 1962 when he was deeply depressed: a whole reduced to a subset.

To think the concept of "set", says Cantor - inventor of the theory of sets (1880) - is to eliminate *the difference of nature* between the elements which compose it[52]. Each element *losing its singularity is* then deprived of *meaning*. Cantor was also a great depressed person...

Now, set theory conceals a paradox that Russell states as follows: "The set of all sets is not a set." How to get out of it? Cantor proposes to introduce a new mathematical concept, that of "multiplicity", while John von Neumann (Neumann János Lajos) will

---

51. Louis ALTHUSSER, *Letters to Franca*, Stock/Imec, Paris, 1998, p. 157-158. Important book. Like the *Confessions* of Jean-Jacques Rousseau. Althusser was an analyst of René Diatkine.
52. Georg CANTOR, "Les principaux concepts de la théorie des ensembles" in *Introduction à l'histoire des sciences*, collection "Classiques Hachette" directed by Georges Canguilhem, Librairie Hachette, Paris, 1970, p. 78. Note that Cantor had the opportunity to work in depth on Spinoza's texts.

5. Listening/dreaming. Therapeutic track

speak of "class[53]". Mathematics, we see it, resists. It is because it has, as Jacques Roubaud says, a therapeutic power: it protects by the impression of certainty that it provides[54]. Like logic. But, isn't this "impression of certainty", necessarily, an *affect*? These affects by definition excluded from mathematics and logic...

Just think of the classical syllogism demonstrating Socrates' mortality: "Socrates is a man. All men are mortal. Therefore Socrates is mortal." Syllogism always represented by an inclusion of sets.

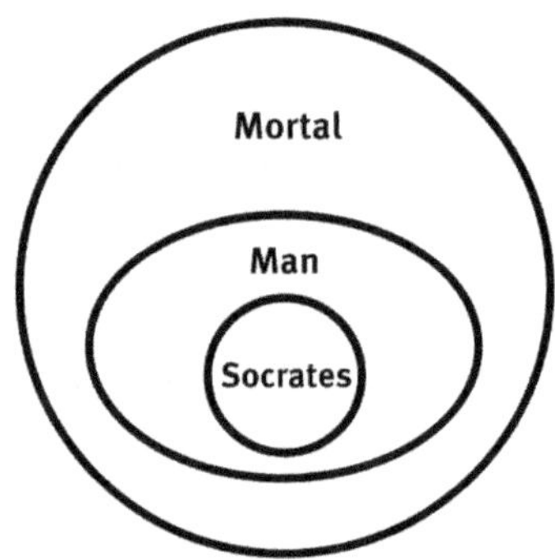

---

53. Nicolas BOURBAKI, *Éléments d'histoire des mathématiques*, Hermann, Paris, 1969, p. 49.
54. Jacques ROUBAUD, *Mathématique : (récit)*, Éditions du Seuil, Paris, 1997, p. 53.

The problem is that this proposition, purely logical and therefore *disaffected,* throws a veil over the essential. The dramatic reality: Socrates had been *sentenced* to death. In the extermination camps, the statement "All men are mortal" was meaningless. The truth of this formula had now passed into another: "All men can be *murdered*[55].

The reality, in the end, is that the "set" of all sets is probably not mathematically possible. It goes beyond logic and escapes it. Let us risk a hypothesis: this totality could be *memory*. At each moment of the present, indeed, it makes a past that it will not cease to totalize.

Bergson evoked the danger to let oneself go "to deduce lazily consequences according to the rules of a rectilinear logic[56] " to which he opposed "the intuition". In the same way, he criticized the philosophies referring to the *time* infiltrated of space which came to them from the "hard sciences", evoking the importance of the *duration*, the lived time. It is however to geometry that he also appeals in *Matter and Memory*

---

55. Günther ANDERS, *The Obsolescence of Man, op. cit.* p. 269-270.
56. Henri BERGSON, "Le possible et le réel" (1930) in *La Pensée et le Mouvant* (1934), Éditions Skira, Geneva, 1946, p. 120.

5. Listening/dreaming. Therapeutic track

to represent the movements that he imagines between "the totality of the memories arranged in AB" and their outcome, the summit of a cone S ("the current perception") where the memories until then "in waiting"[57] crystallize in words.

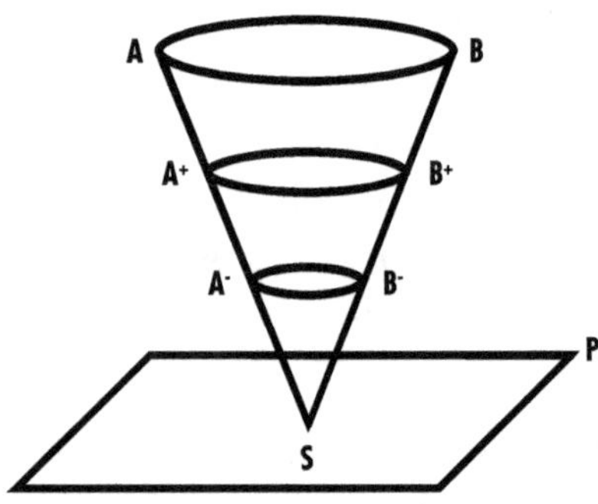

This drawing illustrates a limpid text of *Matter and Memory*. It forgets, however, surprisingly, the essential: *the other*. The way it *affects* us.

Let's keep the pattern. But with a twist.

---

57. *Id, Matter and Memory. Essai sur la relation du corps à l'esprit* (1896), Éditions Skira, Geneva, 1946, p. 157-177. Let us recall that Bergson, as a high school student, had won the first prize in the general mathematics competition.

S represents now the image that an individual can have of himself inside a group (a point in a plan), group whose pressure will go until imposing to him without his knowledge, *when he will associate*, its codes, its stereotyped roles. This representation of himself, ineluctably, provokes a certain *arrangement of his memory*, here reduced to a cone. The circles, sections of the cone at certain moments of its history, have a surface all the more large (are more and more invested of affects) that they go back more far in its past. The biggest part of his memory - and consequently of his associations - was thus stolen from him by this reorganization, necessary to adapt to the other. But, prisoner of the circles which enclose him, it is impossible for him to *understand him*. Freud, in *The Interpretation of Dreams*, speaks of a "circle of thoughts"[58].

Let us return to the depressed philosopher who, to represent his self-image, drew an inclusion of circles. He suffered, like Cantor, from a bipolar manic-depressive disorder. A pathology in which, as we know,

---

58. *Gedankenkreis*: literally "circle of thoughts"; *Vorstellungsgruppe*: "group of representations". Sigmund FREUD, *L'interprétation des rêves*, PUF, Paris, 1971, p. 111 and 255.

the passage from one mood to another can occur with surprising rapidity. Everything happens as if the patients' associations had been preselected, sorted, their *memory* having been successively the object of real *montages (in the cinematographic sense of the term*[59]*)*. What presents itself to them with the intuitive certainty of a totality, of a *whole, is* only a *montage* conditioning all their associations without their knowledge. Sometimes exclusively happy memories, the ideas follow one another at full speed; sometimes, on the contrary, the most damning scenes of their past. A montage thus confirming each time in their manic or melancholic mood.

It is thus not excluded that the bipolar manic-depressive disorder - as was hysteria at the end of the 19th century - allows a renewed understanding of the so-called "psychic" sufferings. Leibniz already, two centuries before, had had the idea of a monad, closed, "without windows". Point of view on the world, world itself. "As *when one turns continuously in the same direction* [...] Memory provides *a kind of*

---

59. Selection of shots from a film (here, sorting of scenes from the past all going in the same *direction*) which will be assembled, *associated* in an order independent of that of time.

consecution to the souls, which imitates reason, but which must be distinguished from it [...] The strong imagination which strikes them and moves them comes either from the greatness, or from the multitude of the preceding perceptions [...][60]." An anticipation of the very concept of "assembly of memory". Memory, this virtual being, singular, invisible and yet giant, so strangely forgotten - except by Proust.

Memory, a palimpsest of montages?

"My brain is a palimpsest and so is yours, reader. Countless layers of ideas, images, feelings have fallen successively on your brain as smoothly as light. It seemed that each one buried the previous one. But none in reality perished."

Charles Baudelaire, *Les Paradis artificiels.*

It is therefore not "sets" that we would find, stratified in the palimpsest of memory, but *montages*[61].

---

60. Gottfried W. Leibniz, *The Monadology*, § 21, § 26 and § 27. Written in 1714, in French (my italics).
61. Let us recall here the perspective of Félix Guattari: "Unlike the logic of the sets, a "machinic" of the arrangements [...] crossed of stratified fields [...] points of singularity [...] crystals of possible [...] rhizomes being able to connect two unspecified

A *theory of montage* could thus be elaborated, which Eisenstein had anticipated. He spoke of "pathetic connections", of the "emotional resonances" that the succession of two images could produce. In a montage, in fact, a "splice", a connection, brings something new and changes everything. Now, this whole is a meaning[62]. Editing, mysteriously, *produces meaning.* Two editors, each making their own choice from the same rushes, will give birth to *two films that are completely different in their very meaning*[63]. Unlike what happens in the "sets", it is the details, the singularities that will make the law here. Snippets that can be bridges that sometimes allow to escape from a montage. It is here that the

---

points [...]", Félix GUATTARI, *L'inconscient machinique. essais de schizo-analyse*, Éditions Recherches, Paris, 1979, p. 9-14.

62. "It is a question of remaking the world in each film, through editing. The expression is by Yann Dedet *in* Dominique VILLAIN, *Le montage au cinéma, op. cit.* p. 20. remake the world. Or to undo it, one should add, since a montage is also capable of "smoothing" a reality, of trivializing it. Aren't television newscasts montages where the "information" is reduced to intercalary shots between news, weather, sports results, *commercials* - and stock market prices?

63. Walter MURCH, *In the Blink of an Eye. Past, present and future of editing*, Capricci, Nantes, 2012, p. 35.

concept of memory, as palimpsest of montages is precious[64].

"None of these metaphors for memory fully satisfied Freud. It was Lou Andreas-Salomé, in 1913, who suggested that cinema, his technique, might well hold the missing piece[65].

Koulechov's montage: private screening

How can a montage produce meaning? The Koulechov effect provides essential elements to try to answer this question. It can be summarized as follows: the *same* close-up of an actor's inexpressive face seems to express sensations or feelings as different

---

64. "Between the *palimpsest* which carries, superimposed one on the other, a Greek tragedy, a monastic legend, and a story of chivalry, and the divine palimpsest created by God, which is *our immeasurable memory*, there is this difference that, in the first, there is a kind of fantastic, grotesque chaos, a collision between heterogeneous elements; whereas, in the second, the fatality of temperament necessarily puts a harmony among the most disparate elements. Charles BAUDELAIRE, *Les Paradis artificiels*, VIII, "Visions d'Oxford", I, "Le Palimpseste" in *Œuvres complètes*, t. I, "Bibliothèque de la Pléiade", Gallimard, Paris, 1980, p. 505.
65. Quoted *in* Jean-Louis BAUDRY, *L'Effet cinéma*, " Ça-cinéma", Éditions Albatros, Paris, 1978, p. 29.

as hunger, sadness or desire, depending on whether, after editing, it immediately follows the image of an appetizing plate, a corpse or a woman "lasciviously lying down"[66].

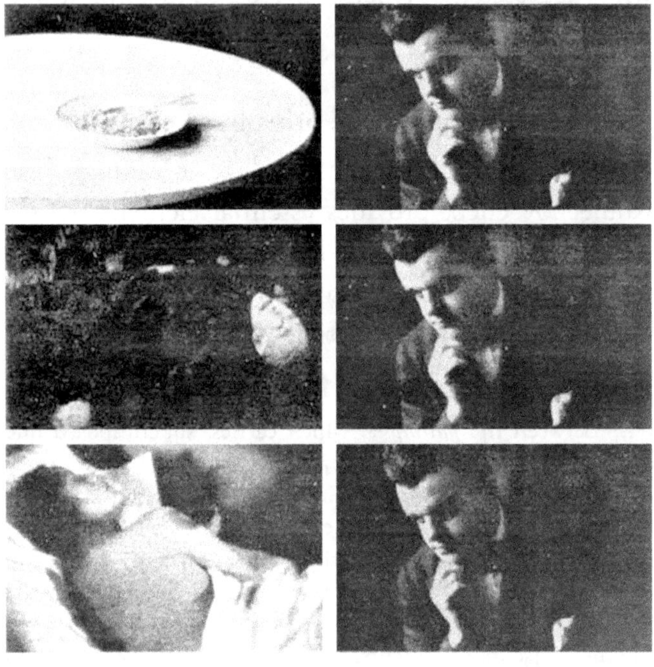

66. "The Koulechov Effect," *Iris,* vol. 4, n° 1, 1986. The Koulechov effect comes from an experiment made in 1920 at the Moscow Film School. See on Internet: https://www.youtube.com/watch?v=7mY1lTz_NPw

It is not by chance that, in Koulechov's example, the second image is that of a look[67]. Koulechov reveals to us what is at stake between two images for the sole reason that they have been connected[68]. Everything happens as if, on the "inexpressive eyes" of the actor (the second image), we were unknowingly *projecting* "something" induced by the previous image. And it is *the eyes which, by becoming a glance*, reveal it to us.

Every encounter is indeed, in a certain way, the occasion of a connection between two images. The first is the image of *the other*, such as we apprehend it in the first moment of the encounter, from a necessarily simplistic idea: "a cop" for example. Will he ask us for our identity papers? The affect, aroused by this

---

67. "To connect on a glance, it is almost the definition of the montage, its supreme ambition at the same time as its subjection to the staging", Jean-Luc Godard quoted *in* Dominique VILLAIN, *Le Montage au cinéma, op. cit.*, p. 126.

68. "It was at this time that I made an editing experiment that is known abroad as the "Koulechov effect". I alternated the same shot of Mosjoukine with various other shots (soup plate, young girl, child's coffin). These shots acquired *a different meaning. The discovery astounded me* and thus I became convinced of the great power of editing", Lev KOULECHOV, "Souvenirs (1918-1920)", *Cahiers du cinéma*, n° 222, July 1970 (my italics). See: https://blogpeda.ac-bordeaux.fr/gmdl/2015/10/16/groupe-comprehension-de-limage/

first image - we already have the impression of being guilty - will be projected onto the second image, the eyes of this "cop", which then become a look. And we begin, in spite of ourselves, to *live* the judgment, *the idea* - we believe, wrongly, to *read* it in his look - that the other makes of us[69].

But this is only possible if our own memory has been the object (just after the perception of the first image) of a real *editing*, since we "feel" it and all our associations confirm it: we *are* guilty.

"A book must be the axe that breaks the frozen sea within us."

Franz Kafka, "Letter to Oskar Pollak," January 27, 1904.

---

69. Concept that Bergson had undoubtedly sensed, when he wrote: "We place ourselves in a certain *disposition*, variable with the interlocutor, variable with the language he speaks, with the kind of ideas he expresses and especially with the general movement of his sentence as if we were beginning to regulate the *tone of* our intellectual work. The motor scheme, underlining his intentions, following, from detour to detour, the *curve of* his thought, shows our thought the *way*. It is the empty container, determining, by its form, the form where tends the fluid mass which rushes there", Henri BERGSON, *Matter and Memory*, *op. cit.* p. 126-127 (my italics).

"I don't know well where I am anymore, nor where the pieces of my life are [...] I also struggle with old obstacles that block my view and make me despair[70]." Because it is a *prison without walls*, a montage of memory can indeed be the most subtle, the strangest of incarcerations. The infernal huis clos imagined by Sartre is almost naive, beside. Its disadvantage, especially, is to suggest that no escape is possible. A montage, one can get out of it.

A montage is all the more insistent, however, all the more deadly, that it has been able to revive an old connection, a "childhood sticker" all impregnated with the first affects - often a guilt. This is how a conventional *meaning* - "a cop" - can become, through the intermediary, after the blossoming of a look, a singular *meaning*, ours. This is the secret of certain connections, sometimes surprisingly dangerous, because they create meaning. A continuity until then latent that a sudden *affect* makes *live*[71]. "To feel", one

---

70. Louis Althusser, *Letters to Franca*, op. cit., p. 546 and 547.
71. Gaston Bachelard, *La dialectique de la durée*, PUF, Paris, 2001, p. 113: "What makes continuity is always an obscure dialectic that calls for feelings about impressions, memories about sensations." And, p. 116: "The musical action is discontinuous.

5. Listening/dreaming. Therapeutic track

says. To feel "beautiful" or "ugly", "young" or "old", "man" or "woman", or even "French" in England, is in the end, to be *conscious of a role* in the human comedy, where the *dominant mythology* maintained by the publicity[72] distributes the "beautiful" and the "bad" roles.

The words that exclude by the assemblies they operate

"Life, all of life is a set-up."
Antonin Artaud.

Thus, it is in the form of an affective color, of a *mood*, that a latent associative assembly is revealed and that *an image* of ourselves is imposed on us at the moment when, in front of us, eyes have become

---

It is our sentimental resonance that brings it continuity."
72. Moreover, Biotherm admits that men's formulas are often a little more muscular [...] Women have obtained a lot," summarized Nicolas Trussardi. It's up to the man to make up for it by increasing his seduction through a somewhat savage virility [...] Men's skin care products promote "punchy" titles. Today, men dare to use their own products. On the condition that these products do not threaten his virility, his sexual prowess, by a too "cosmetic" argument [...]"; see the "Supplement" of the newspaper *Le Monde* of September 25, 1999.

a look. We cannot say it enough, this image is most often only a cliché, a stereotype in progress in a certain group, a job in a certain troupe of actors. And it is undoubtedly this presence, more or less conscious, of a collective, of a clan - one is recognized or excluded from it - that affects most painfully.

"You're ugly, do us a favor [we'll note the *we*], kill yourself!", had read, one day, on a "social network" a teenager - before killing herself[73]. In the *Daily Mail* of August 7, 2013, one could discover the photo of four teenagers who had committed suicide in this way. Probably because they had not been given the weapons that allow them to resist the words, to unmask the murderous clichés of a pack[74]. For it was words that prepared all the massacres. Words that described "the physique of Jews", for example, before exterminating them. The same words, but those of the Great Lakes in East Africa, blown by the colonists in Rwanda and Burundi at the beginning of the 20th century and anchored in the indigenous minds, stigmatized the Tutsis ("their noses, their ears") on the

---

73. Pascale Krémer, "Une adolescente sur cinq a déjà tenté de se suicider," lemonde.fr, February 5, 2014.
74. http://www.lepoint.fr/monde/le-site-ask-fm-dans-le- collimator-after-multiple-teen-suicides- 09-08-2013-1712786_24.php

5. Listening/dreaming. Therapeutic track

radio of the Thousand Hills before Hutu extremists proceeded to their genocide.

How does one come to feel "Black" in front of a White man, "Jewish" in front of an anti-Semite, "Tutsi" in front of a Hutu? It is here that the concept of montage is precious. A montage, objective, can be contagious, suggests Eisenstein. What *emerges from* the *simple linking of two shots* of a film sets in motion (*e-meets*), spreads like a wave that *will rise* the memory of a spectator. Eisenstein brings this process closer to the actor's work of interpretation. He evokes "the *internal* technique by which the actor comes to feel, to be *possessed* by a living feeling that will unfold in the authenticity of his behavior on stage or on screen[75] ". A method that consists, according to him (Eisenstein was also an excellent actor), in imagining a set, details representing various aspects of the situation to be played. A courtroom, for example, an

75. Sergei Mikhailovich EISENSTEIN, *The film: its form, its meaning*, Christian Bourgois éditeur, Paris, 1976, p. 229. Eisenstein adds: "The principle of editing in cinema is only a partial application *of the principle of editing in general.*" It is probably not indifferent to note that all that concerned the development, by Eisenstein, of this idea was *omitted* in the Soviet edition of "Works of S.M. Eisenstein".

"accusing" objective montage, can, by generating a subjective montage, lead a being - or an actor working on his role - to "feel guilty[76]".

And one thinks here of the mad anger of Artaud. Anger provoked by those who "parade now in front of Van Gogh to whom, during his life, they or their fathers and mothers, have so well twisted the neck[77]". Artaud, still, speaking about the beings to which one closed the mouth: "Because one was afraid that their poetry does not leave the books and does not reverse the reality[78]." Their poetry or their philosophy. Spinoza.

Spinoza had been excommunicated by the synagogue. Excluded by the excluded. Jewish squared, in a way. More "Jewish", in short, than Mortera the rabbi who had excommunicated him. Spinoza's opponents were not mistaken when they called him "the Jew of Amsterdam". Reversing reality: the necessary condition for survival when one is the victim of a *double exclusion*. As if being born into an

----

76. Essential process of which we will be brought to specify the mechanism.
77. Antonin ARTAUD, *Van Gogh, le suicidé de la société*, Gallimard, Paris, 2001, p. 94.
78. *Ibid*, p. 10.

5. Listening/dreaming. Therapeutic track

environment of outcasts conferred the painful advantage of acquiring certain defensive reflexes from the cradle. Those which will allow later to dismantle the codes which oppose a singularity whatever it is. This was the case for Spinoza, but also to a certain extent for Ludwig Börne[79], that little-known person we will talk about again, or more recently for Annie Ernaux, Didier Eribon, Édouard Louis. And of course for Pierre Bourdieu. These defectors who got out of it by becoming bilingual. They tell us, shout at us, that to exclude is to seek to kill. But that the excommunicated can survive if he manages to *dismantle* the false evidence of the dominant set-ups.

II. Dismantling an excommunication: Spinoza's analysis

"I will explain in what sense I sometimes lost all hope. But Spinoza always *cured* me, and very quickly.
Alain, *History of my thoughts.*

---

79. Ludwig Börne is the pseudonym he had chosen for himself "to finish with Judah Löb Baruch" he could have said, paraphrasing in advance a title of Édouard Louis.

Spinoza's coat filmed by Eisenstein

A fanatic does not support that one criticizes the dogma where he found the treatment of his anguish. The group that has given him an identity. In 1656, in Amsterdam, one evening, Spinoza, 24 years old, coming out of the Portuguese synagogue, was confronted by an individual who threatened him with his dagger. A step aside and Spinoza avoids the blow which will only tear his clothes. He would keep the pierced coat all his life. Shortly afterwards, he was excommunicated. In murderous terms[80].

The text of this excommunication (*Herem*) must be reread. Its structure: "1. *the said Spinoza* has been found guilty; 2. *we* exclude him, drive him out, curse him, and abhor him; 3. *you* must not have any relationship with him, either written or verbal. Let no one come within four cubits of him. Each of these terms was repeated in a haunting way, in a certain *rhythm*.

---

80. The same year (1656) curiously, in France, a royal edict created the "General Hospital", which would not be a simple refuge, "but rather a moral institution charged with chastising, correcting a certain moral "vacancy", which does not deserve the court of men, but could not be rectified by the only severity of penance". This creation *thus substituted the confinement* to the *exclusion*: see Michel FOUCAULT, *History of the madness to the classic age*, Gallimard, Paris, 1976, p. 86.

5. Listening/dreaming. Therapeutic track

A text surprisingly reminiscent, by its structure, of the murderous Facebook message we mentioned. A judgment, a condemnation where the *we* is present, the punishment. A montage. There again intended to provoke in its victim a rearrangement of all the being from a modification of its image in its own eyes. This image so dependent on a *us*.

I saw myself," writes Spinoza, "in extreme peril and forced to seek with all my strength a remedy, even if it were uncertain, just as a patient suffering from a fatal disease, *sensing his certain death* if a remedy is not applied to him, is forced to seek it with all his strength [...][81] " For it is life that is at stake here. Hegel had felt it, who spoke of a "struggle to death between two consciences". This death is "dishonor". Honor" indeed confers a certain self-image but makes one dependent on others, says Spinoza. This is how *words can kill*.

The art of not committing suicide - in fact not letting oneself be killed - consists in opposing them with other words. To try to say *oneself*, to rebuild *oneself* through a refusal.

---

81. Baruch SPINOZA, *Traité de la réforme de l'entendement*, GF/Flammarion, Paris, 2003, p. 69 (my italics).

To escape from this evil illusion trick, it is essential to dismantle it. Starting with the speech that accompanies it, the pitch.

Spinoza's resistance. His accent. Landing on the "Philosophy continent

There is nothing more deterritorialized, more exotic than the little Baruch that Deleuze loved so much. Thus, it is on a boat that one reads it best. What did Henri Landier, the engraver who speaks about it so well. And my father.

Having a torn coat could also be speaking a language with a *foreign* accent. A wounded language, cause of shame. But perhaps a source of enrichment. The trace of something *else*. The memory of a journey. In the Yiddish songs, the music seems to listen to the pain of the words. Baruch will keep this cloak all his life as if to make sure he never forgets its tear. The fear in front of the other, the surprise, in front of so much hatred. The need, while keeping his singularity, his *accent*, to never relax his vigilance[82]. And the warning that one day it will be necessary to take the road again.

---

82. *Caute* ("Be vigilant"): Spinoza's motto.

Alone, taking refuge in an island that is not on any map (biographers lose track of him between 1656, the date of his excommunication, and 1661), Spinoza, no doubt at the price of hard work on himself, managed to leave a mode that made him suffer and to find a lost substance - his freedom. The *Ethics*, generously, will reveal to us the paths he had to blaze, he for whom "the authority of Plato, Aristotle, Socrates, etc., did not carry much weight".[83]

The *Ethics*, by its radical novelty, tells of a landing. The continent is philosophy. An occupied territory. Invaded by the theology of the time. The risk is immense. The pyres are never far away. Never mind, we will take care of the preparation. A logistical organization which will have to be without defect, *more geometrico*. Spinoza learns Latin and reads Descartes. "Before, I was thought. Now I am thinking. *And* I am" he could have said after this attentive, implacable reading of Descartes, the man who "went forward masked".

One morning, Spinoza's forces are dropped on five different philosophical beaches with the mission to

---

83. Baruch SPINOZA, "letter to Hugo Boxel" in *Œuvres complètes*, " Bibliothèque de la Pléiade ", Gallimard, Paris, 1967, p. 1247.

make a junction on the fifth one, called "On human freedom", the most advanced. The first wave, skilfully camouflaged, succeeds in turning the defense of the other side and, to top it all, in installing a bridgehead in the heart of the opposing fortress: *God*. This takeover is part of the famous "By God, I mean (*intelligo*)[84] [...]" where from the outset, in a few words, Baruch, torpedoing the headquarters, reconquers a territory hitherto controlled by the enemy. This operation is strangely reminiscent of the battle with the angel, after which Jacob changed his name. Israel means "the one who has fought with God"[85]. A hand-to-hand combat from which even Descartes, though so courageous, had shied away. The second wave then attacked the bastion of *knowledge*. The third one ventures on a mined ground to which philosophers until then had forbidden themselves the access: *affectivity*. All that remains is to unmask, before the last assault, the hidden source of all *powers*. And it is the landing, on the beach of *freedom*, of a commando

---

84. "By God I mean an absolutely infinite being, that is, a substance consisting of an infinity of attributes, each of which expresses an eternal and infinite essence", Baruch SPINOZA, *Ethics*, I: "On God - Definition VI".
85. ישראל, in Hebrew.

equipped with the new weapon, *knowledge/understanding*. Its flag is a book: *Ethics*.

Ethics: understanding to de-alter oneself

"How I love this honest man

More than words can say

Yet fear that he remains alone

With its radiant halo.

"You must forgive me with kindness

If I think here of Münchhausen

Which, unique in its kind, succeeds

To pull itself out of the swamp, by its own braid.

"You think his example shows us

This is what this doctrine can give to men.

Don't be fooled by the reassuring appearance:

One must be born for the sublime."

Albert Einstein, *About Spinoza's* Ethics[86].

All reading is projective. We put what we think to the test of what we read. Baruch's astonishing "modernity": he resists and even enriches concepts

---

86. Albert EINSTEIN, *Œuvres choisies*, t. V "Sciences, Éthique, Philosophie", Éditions du Seuil/CNRS, Paris, 1991, p. 247-248. This is an excerpt from a poem written probably around 1920.

invented several centuries after his death, notably those of Freud. It is as if he had invented a machine for eternal understanding. For the real question, in the end, is: *what is understanding*[87]? A term whose meaning is crucial for the whole of *Ethics*, says Macherey[88].

The reason why the three hundred pages of the *Ethics* still shed such a dazzling light on us is because of the fourth and fifth definitions in the first part. Perhaps they can only be really understood when one is in *a certain mood*, as one sometimes is, for example, when one is coming out of a dream. At the moment when a bit of reality is fleetingly seized.

At the beginning of the *Ethics* are in fact successively defined: substance, attributes and modes. It is only with the *mode* that *the other* appears in the book. And at the same time, with it, *the affect*. "By mode I understand the *affections* of the substance, that is to say that which is in *another thing* [*in alio*]

---

87. In order to *understand* Descartes, Spinoza had to *listen to him* intensely: he had to accept to identify himself transitorily with him, before finding himself. Not quite the same.
88. Pierre MACHEREY, *Introduction to Spinoza's* Ethics. *La cinquième partie. Les voies de la libération*, PUF, Paris, 1997, p. 134.

5. Listening/dreaming. Therapeutic track

through which it is also conceived[89]. The torn coat, thus, was for Spinoza the way in which *substance*, one day, through one of its attributes, had been dramatically affected. A trace that nothing will erase.

It happens that a scar remains painful. *Founding* pain if it is the starting point of a process aiming to overcome fear, to deliver from imposed roles, to disconcert false destinies. To *de-alter* oneself. *A* necessary condition if we want to find what Spinoza calls *substance*[90]. Sub-stance, invisible *underneath* which sub-sists, and which is really cause of itself (*causa sui*). Now, it is from the most singular thing that we can access it. By passing from the idea of this thing to the reality of the reasons for which it affected us. To its *meaning*. The way to a knowledge of the third kind.

From affects to the knowledge of the third gender

"What bothers me about the *Ethics* is that the experience it calls for, the experience it makes possible

---

89. Baruch Spinoza, *Ethics*, I, "Definition V".
90. "By substance I mean that which is in itself and is conceived by itself, that is, that whose concept does not need the concept of another thing in order to be formed", Baruch Spinoza, *Ethics*, I, 3.

in a purely theoretical way, does not seem to me to be attainable by a man. In any case, it has never been given to me, and I doubt that it has ever been given to anyone.
Ferdinand Alquié, *Lessons on Spinoza*.

Spinoza opposes the *active* affects to the passions, the *passive* affects. The primary active affects, the joy, the sadness attest the increase or the decrease of "the force to exist", to persevere in its being. To dare to be. To dare to assume, to make exist in act its singular essence. By giving him a *sense*[91]. Still it is necessary to have its own imaginary, of all its potential associations. To reappropriate its affects by depassioning them[92].

The love-passion, the hatred are indeed *altered* affects, undergone, accidental, bound to the representation that one makes of a certain *other*. A passion (etymologically, a *suffering*) can thus *alienate* by subordinating a being to the law of the other, to his look. A glance on which, in reality - Koulechov

---

91. Baruch Spinoza, *Ethics*, V, 39.
92. Pierre Macherey, *Introduction to Spinoza's* Ethics. *La cinquième partie. Les voies de la libération, op. cit.* p. 56-57 and 68-71.

effect -, one projects the assembly of memory of which one had become captive.

If we imagine - wrongly - as absolutely free this external object, we can be led to fetishize it in the form of a passion or a hate. Madness whose source is undoubtedly a forgotten history. That of the trusting glance of the former small child in us: the "imaginary crystallization" dear to Stendhal[93].

To escape from a passion, the awareness of a causality to which the object of this passion would itself be subjected is not enough. It is necessary moreover that is found the free sequence of our ideas. In short, to escape from a fascinated assembly. To the knowledge of the second kind (by the concepts), the *knowledge of the third kind* associates, as we have seen, the "intuition" of a *singular thing*, as far as this singularity *affects* us. The *knowledge/understanding* reconciles thus rationality and affectivity. Meaning and sense. Light *and* heat.

A dream can help to get out of these confinements. To finish with their latent violence. In the

---

93. "What I call crystallization, it is the operation of the spirit which draws from all that presents itself the discovery that the beloved object has new perfections", STENDHAL, *De l'amour*, Garnier-Flammarion, Paris, 1965, p. 35.

Recherche, one night, Swann, in search of Odette, dreams that he is walking with a young man in a fez and Napoleon III. In this dream - which is not devoid of humor - it is no longer Forcheville who has taken Odette from him, it is Napoleon III. At the same time, he is replaced in his role by the unknown and weeping young man. That very morning, after associating with these unusual characters, Swann came out of his unhappy love, out of his jealousy, and "de-odetted" himself.[94]

The knowledge of the third kind. A primer on affectivity in the world of value

Every morning, in front of a mirror, a staging of the body image takes place. Everything is done to protect one's appearance from the glances that one will encounter during the day.

Who is looking? We can ask ourselves this when we contemplate ourselves in a mirror, because *it is with the words of others* that we describe ourselves - "Oh, these cheeks! - and that, meticulously, conscientiously,

---

94. Marcel PROUST, *Du côté de chez Swann*, in *À la recherche du temps perdu*, t. I, "Bibliothèque de la Pléiade", Gallimard, Paris, 1987, reprinted 1991, p. 372-375.

we try to repair childhood wounds. A make-up. It is indeed on the body itself that the secret alphabet of affectivity is inscribed. The inscription of caresses or old slaps. The first joys, the first sadnesses. An alphabet of affects which will not cease to be invisibly recreated with the wire of the assemblies induced by the succession of the meetings. Such could be the meaning of Anders' sentence placed in epigraph of the present book: "We are quite simply illiterates of anguish."

Know/understand. To associate. But, so that this movement unties affectivity, generates sense, it is essential that it does not let itself be diverted by misleading cultural, philosophical associations-screens, for example[95]. They only attest in fact the ignored presence of a group, of its codes. And whether we

---

95. It is in this way that the teaching of philosophy, which competitions "sanction", can constitute a real obstacle to a Spinozian knowledge of the third kind. A ban on thinking. Each idea is in fact immediately "associated" with quotations, references, referring to "great philosophical texts". These screen associations thus only oppose any free association. Fortunately, there are professors who trace the struggle of certain individuals who, for reasons of their own, decided to tear themselves away from the received ideas of their time. And to rethink them radically. Philosophically. There is no quotation in Spinoza's *Ethics*.

like it or not, the surreptitious introduction of the "virus of the value[96]". Because the sense is, very early, contaminated by the value. In the history of an individual, the desire to be simply loved implies indeed very quickly that to see *recognized* a certain image of oneself. A place in the world of the value.

The virus of *value* thus introduces its hierarchies even into emotional impulses: "He's my best friend...", "Who do you prefer?" The very desire is parasitized by value judgments: "beauty", social prestige. Just think of the young African women for whom "skin whitening" is still a frequent practice: "When you are light, you have more flirts...[97]"

Pascal, already, had described this ambiguous attraction for a being whose "value" would be able to value the one he loves[98]. What comes to fan, we will

---

96. See p. 61ff.

97. http://www.slateafrique.com/93979/abidjan-les-ravages-du-blanchiment

98. "Whoever loves someone because of his beauty, does he love him? No, because the smallpox that will kill the beauty without killing the person, will make him not love her anymore. And if I am loved for my judgment, for my memory, will I be loved? No, because I can lose these qualities without losing myself. Let no one, therefore, mock those who are honored for offices and positions, for *no one is loved except for borrowed qualities*," Blaise

5. Listening/dreaming. Therapeutic track

return to it, the affective mimicry: "If we imagine that the men love something or hate it, we will love it or we will hate it[99]". Carried by an operative thought impregnated of the dominant mythology, by the history that it tells surreptitiously, the roles that it assigns to us, stereotypes invade until the language of the desire. It is then that the dream intervenes. This strange story which holds the way of a possible deliverance.

III. Dismantling the narratives that hold us captive

"The adaptation of certain patients to reality contributes to giving the change because, like mental activity, it is essentially practical, *operative*, and does not correspond to an effective libidinal investment [...] The phantasmal magma of early childhood, a *mixture of sensations and affects, foreign to logic*, is in them kept at a distance and, if not lost, as absent."

Pierre Marty, Michel de M'Uzan, Christian David, *L'investigation psychosomatique.*

Pascal quoted in Pierre MACHEREY, *Identités*, De L'Incidence Éditeur, Saint-Vincent-de-Mercuze (38660), 2013, pp. 93-94 (my emphasis).
99. Baruch SPINOZA, *Ethics*, III, 29, demonstration.

Operative thinking and associative thinking. Another narrative is possible

"You smile at the absurdity of your dream and at the same time you have the feeling that this jumble of extravagances encloses a kind of thought, a real thought belonging to your present life, something that exists and has always existed in your heart."

Fyodor Mikhailovich Dostoyevsky, *The Idiot.*

Strange, intimate *encounter*, a dream every night shows us that another narration is possible, different from those in which we are caught. Freud then suggests us to apply to the dream a method, that of free association. Now, "the fundamental rule" of this method - to let *anything* come to mind - implies a decisive choice: *the abandonment of any value judgment.* A *revolutionary* choice: from the start, everything is played out[100]. An *associative thought* can be deployed, different from the *operative* thought, this purely logical step[101]. The dream is not, in fact,

---

100. Max DORRA, "For a Dreaming of Understanding," *Chimeras*, no. 86, 2015, p. 23.
101. "There is something frozen, dead, in all operative thought, including psychoanalytic thought," J.-B. PONTALIS, *Between Dream and Pain*, "Knowledge of the Unconscious," Gallimard,

5. Listening/dreaming. Therapeutic track

a police enigma answering to a *logical causality*, but an unedited story governed by an *associative causality* carrying *meaning*, this word so overused. It should be noted that Spinoza, an astonishing precursor, had explicitly made the difference between the two modes of thought[102].

The *operative thought*[103] has as requirement to put aside the affectivity of the individuals, to forget the keyboard of their memory, in the pretext of the "objectivity", of the efficiency, of the speed that the world of the value requires. A world to which it is not easy to resist, so much the narratives in which it encloses us, omnipresent, blow us without that we are always conscious of it their images and their words.

Paris, 1977, p. 47. There is, however, incredible resistance to the idea of engaging in associative thought. Freud, twenty years after the publication of the *interpretation of dreams*, spoke of "stubborn incomprehension".

102. Baruch Spinoza, *Ethics*, II, 18, scolie: "I say that this enchainment is done according to the order and sequence of the affections of the human body, in order to distinguish it from the enchainment of ideas, which is done according to the order of the understanding; the latter enables the mind to perceive things by their first causes and is the same in all men."

103. Pierre Marty, Michel de M'Uzan, Christian David, *L'investigation psychosomatique*, PUF, Paris, 1963.

However, because of the efficiency of digital technology, programming is now taught at school. This teaching is justified as long as we keep in mind the characteristics of the algorithmic approach[104] : a strict obedience to an ordered sequence of simple "instructions", excluding any contradiction. A mechanic which is in fact only the skeleton of rationality. It lacks the flesh, which allows a thought - Descartes' was an example - to *tear itself away from* the erroneous discourses of opinion, from the grip of beliefs.

Indeed, even in the most scientific "thought experiments", an associative phase is indispensable. Einstein: "The emotional basis of this combinatorial game seems to be the essential feature of productive thought [...] Conventional words must be laboriously sought only in a second stage, when the *associative game* mentioned is sufficiently established [...][105]", "Invention is not the work of logical thought, even

---

104. The fact that the curious expression "artificial intelligence" is an oxymoron, that digitalization is too often overused, should not make us ignore the tremendous interest of this technological advance. *We must reclaim the digital world.*
105. Albert EINSTEIN, "letter to Jacques Hadamard", June 17, 1944, in *Œuvres choisies*, t. IV, Éditions du Seuil/CNRS, Paris, 1989, p. 129 (my italics).

5. Listening/dreaming. Therapeutic track

if the final product is inseparable from a logical formatting[106]."

Associative thought, thus, is a non-operational thought, as there are non-Euclidean geometries which, by *enveloping* the Euclidean, demonstrate that it is only one geometry among others. Again, it must be said that "free" association only gives back to memory its life, its circulation, if we have previously unmasked the set-ups that insidiously restrict its freedom. Let us recall that this idea - this method - had been more or less consciously inspired to Freud by the reading of Ludwig Börne. In *The Art of Becoming an Original Writer in Three Days,* we read: "A shameful cowardice holds us all back from thinking. There is a censorship far more oppressive than that of governments, it is that of public opinion [...] It is not of spirit but of character that most writers lack [...] Whoever *listens to the voice of his heart instead* of *the noise of the market* and has the courage to propagate what his heart teaches him, he is always original [...] Here is the promised recipe. Write for three consecutive days, without falsification

---

106. *Id.* in "Documents autobiographiques", *Œuvres choisies,* t. V, *op. cit.* p. 14.

or hypocrisy, *everything that comes into your head*, you will be amazed to see how many new thoughts, never before expressed, have sprung up in you [...][107]" It is striking that the same Ludwig Börne, the precursor of the free association method, was also a revolutionary who influenced Engels and Bakunin. Speaking of "the war of the poor against the aristocracy of money [...]", he declared: "Never has a prince given or given back freedom; the people who desire it must conquer it. Nothing is given to those who wait[108] [...]" Ludwig Börne was a curious man: "The deconstruction of himself that he had undertaken ended up forming his identity. He could not stand words or the valuing of his *self* [...][109]"

All in all, two modes of thought - operative (the limit form of rationality) and associative - are essentially different. Yet it is undoubtedly the intertwining

---

107. Ludwig Börne, "L'art de devenir un écrivain original en trois jours" in *Littoral 2, La main du rêve*, Éditions Érès, October 1981, p. 157 to 159.
108. "Letters from Paris," November 19, 1831, *in* Maximilien Rubel, "Introduction" to Karl Marx, *Œuvres,* t. III, "Philosophie," "Bibliothèque de la Pléiade," Gallimard, Paris, 1982, p. XLI (my italics).
109. Rachid L'Aoufir, *Ludwig Börne (1786-1837). Un parisien pas comme les autres.* L'Harmattan, Paris, 2004, p. 34-35.

5. Listening/dreaming. Therapeutic track

of the two approaches that is indispensable when one tries to access the knowledge of the third kind that Spinoza evokes.

Certain philosophical statements have crossed the centuries: "One never bathes in the same river twice"; "Man is a wolf to man[110]". If these words, permanently attached to the names of Heraclitus and Hobbes, have one day disappeared, it is because their meaning was carried by something else. A rhythm, the irruption of a river, a wolf. In short, the emergence of an associative, metaphorical thought, capable of reminding philosophical rationality of the forgotten place of affect. To make it dream.

During an encounter, in the course of exchanges, the associative waves of the other obviously remain unknown to us even though it is our melody that arouses them. Thus are sometimes involuntarily provoked unexpected dissonances, unpredictable mood swings, which would remain unexplained if we did not evoke, in the other, a virtual harmony

---

110. The first part of the sentence is curiously never quoted: "And certainly it is equally true, and that man is a god to man, and that man is also a wolf to man", Thomas HOBBES, *The Citizen* (1642), Librairie générale française, Paris, 1996, p. 53.

unknown to us - stemming from its singular history - that our music went to wake up. Like a sonata for two keyboards where each of the pianists would ignore the notes of the left hand, the secret *accompaniment*, which nevertheless gives its depth to the melody of the other. One always forgets this accompaniment of any meeting: *two invisible children* and yet face to face, each one taken in an irreducibly different history.

We must learn to listen. Spinoza speaks of "idea of idea". One can, in front of the other - a patient, for example - *associate on his associations*. Letting him or her hear it through the quality of a silence could be a way of finding together a little common substance under radically different stories. To reopen to him, with the taste of the crossroads, the field of possibilities that he did not suspect. No longer having the impression of being a simple screen for the interpretations, or even the projections of the listener, he could then, sometimes, *finally feel heard.* Let us think of J.-B. Pontalis' account when he evokes - without explicitly naming him - certain important moments of Georges Perec's analysis[111]. For a long

---

111. J.-B. PONTALIS, *Entre le rêve et la douleur,* "Connaissance de

5. Listening/dreaming. Therapeutic track

time they had been for each other the perfect analy-
sand (dreaming, associating...) and the wise analyst
(interpreting only with good sense...). *Roles*, in spite
of everything, to a certain extent. And then, one day,
something happened. Between their personal stories,
as if the films had finally been set to music, someone
found a way. A mother, perhaps...

The dream and the film: editing, projection

"Projection. It is always a question of rejecting
outside what one refuses to recognize in oneself or to
be oneself."

Jean Laplanche and J.-B. Pontalis, *Vocabulaire de la
psychanalyse*, "Projection".

How good it feels to be in a dark room! The music
of a film often seems to be in complicity with our
secret emotional melody. But it also enters, at the
same time, in resonance with something else, another
music, silent, that of the editing. Any film, thus,

l'inconscient", Gallimard, Paris, 1977, p. 263 and *Perdre de vue*,
"Connaissance de l'inconscient", Gallimard, Paris, 1988, p. 163.
To read, in parallel with Perec's account of his analysis: Georges
Perec, "Les lieux d'une ruse", in *Penser/Classer*, Hachette, Paris,
1986, p. 59-72.

seems caught between two invisible strata: its music and its editing. Two flows. A rhythm. A heartbeat, says Godard. Modulations too, like so many changes of mood. To watch a film is to slip between these two sheets, to enter into the skin of actors dancing to a tune that only they cannot hear.

A montage, such is the structure common to a film and a dream. The "dream worker", of whom Freud speaks, is an editor. When he speaks of "condensation", Freud uses the image of Francis Galton's "composite photos" (overprinted). His friend Fliess evokes "an assembly of all memories". Current digitalization techniques - video editing, virtual editing (especially "inlays") - would undoubtedly authorize many other metaphors.

Walter Murch, Coppola's editor, confides that he rarely dreams while editing a film. "The film monopolizes the dream part of my mind." It's when he's finished editing that the dreams, "impatient up to that point," manifest themselves, he says. Murch likens the director-editor relationship to what happens between a patient recounting a dream and the analyst listening. The dream and the montage, for example, through their choices, their connections, sometimes reveal their secret at the very moment

5. Listening/dreaming. Therapeutic track

when *they defend themselves* against the interpretation that is proposed[112].

Eisenstein went so far as to assert, as we have seen, that montage in cinema was only a particular case of the principle of montage in general. As if the concept of montage was a real *a priori form*. Under this angle, certain notions commonly used in psychoanalysis would then become clearer. That of "projection" in particular, which is not reduced to the ensemblist definition that is usually given: "What is presupposed in the psychoanalytical definition of the projection: a *bipartition* of the part of oneself that is refused[113]. For, what we "project", in reality, is not a simple part, a subset of ourselves, but, as we have seen, a whole reorganization, a real invisible montage of our memory. An assembly where the operative thought

112. Walter Murch, *In the Blink of an Eye. Past, Present and Future of Editing*, *op. cit.* p. 50. "Walter Murch, editor of a Coppola film: 'I don't think an editor can impose a vision on a film that didn't already exist. All the remarks you made were already in Francis Coppola's *head* in one form or another" *in* Michael Ondaatje, *Conversations with Walter Murch. The Art of Film Editing*, Ramsay, Paris, 2009, p. 48.
113. Jean Laplanche, J.-B. Pontalis, *Vocabulaire de la psychanalyse*, "Projection", PUF, Paris, 1971, p. 350 (my italics).

unrolls a logic that it believes to be free whereas it is only the logic of an invisible narrative.

From the story considered as a machine to influence. Objective and subjective montages

"In reality TV studios, as on the video game console, on cell phone and computer screens, from the bedroom to the car, everyday life is permanently *wrapped in a narrative net* [...]"

Christian Salmon, "Une machine à fabriquer des histoires" in *Le Monde diplomatique*, November 2006.

From Greek mythology and the sacred texts of religions to television and the Internet, we live the history of the world through a world of stories. Stories whose formidable capacity to arouse emotions depends on the choice of certain details and even more on their *editing*[114]. The effectiveness of these narratives, of these *machines to influence* in which we bathe, thus determines almost irresistibly our mood, our representation of the world and even our electoral

---

114. Sergei Mikhailovich Eisenstein, in *Cahiers du Cinéma*, n° 222, July 1970.

5. Listening/dreaming. Therapeutic track

choices, sometimes[115]. The affects that a narrative and its connections can arouse are indeed of a formidable contagiousness.

Tell me a story! It is what, from childhood, we ask. One could even conceive, antiphrasing Foucault, an "archaeology of the non-knowledge", of the ignorance, going back to the childhood: a doll, a gendarme, a thief, these apparently innocent games (Monopoly, him, eats squarely the piece) which prepare insidiously the denial of conflicting social realities, disturbing[116].

The media are taking over, especially television, where viewers spend an average of more than three hours a day worldwide. But also, of course, video games. Everything that can give the illusion

---

115. "The success of *storytelling* is not limited to corporate management and marketing; in ten years it has imposed itself on all institutions to the point of appearing as the paradigm of the *cultural revolution of capitalism*, a new narrative norm that irrigates and shapes the most diverse sectors of activity", Christian SALMON, "Une machine à fabriquer des histoires", *Le Monde diplomatique*, November 2006.
116. The stubborn persistence of male domination, for example. Or the fact that the majority of the inmates in the prisons are poor. Poor people who, even now, when they are workers, live seven years less than executives.

of "re-enchanting life". The insidious *emotional mimicry*[117] helping, millions of beings live by proxy loves, joys, sadnesses, angers. All the emotional melody transmitted to them by the actors of the television series or video games they have become addicted to. An emotional mimicry that originates in early childhood[118]. A particularly dangerous process when it transmits violence, the feeling of an aggressive certainty: *ein Volk, ein Reich, ein Führer!*

Now, these narrative discourses contain, pre-selected, infiltrated by the operative thought, stereotyped characters - stereotypes impregnated with ideology - from which the image that we have of ourselves will be nourished. Our "narrative identity", would say Ricœur. It is by inducing a role that the objective assembly of a narrative can generate a subjective assembly which without our knowledge assigns us a destiny. Fate seeming all the more inescapable that it will have been more infiltrated by an operative thought, excluding the analogical thus deprived of

---

117. "In describing this "contagion of feelings", Spinoza anticipated the discovery of the "mirror neurons" *in* Max DORRA, *Lutte des rêves et interprétation des classes. Dismantling a trick of illusion, op. cit.* p. 133.
118. Baruch SPINOZA, *Ethics*, III, proposition 32, scolie.

5. Listening/dreaming. Therapeutic track

metaphors. A judgment without appeal. Double secret, here again: the *ignored* horizontality of the narrative in which we are taken and the *unconscious* associative verticality that affects it.

The revolutionary events themselves were often lived by their actors through an imaginary inherited from the past, remarked Marx[119]. The French Revolution, in spite of its radical novelty, was played out in Roman costume, with Roman phrases. Then, the stories of 1789 will haunt the mind of the insurgents of 1848. The Commune of Paris finally, the Cuban and Chinese revolutions will be constantly present in the head and the word of the Parisian soixante-huitards. There is thus a real *struggle of the narratives*. Even in everyday life. The "Harlequin" collection, much more widely read than the works of the Marquis de Sade, is in this respect infinitely more toxic. What is it to be "a boy", "a girl", "a black man", or "the son of a cleaning lady", if not a never-ending struggle against reductive identifications. A fight where our freedom is at stake.

---

119. Karl MARX, *Le 18 Brumaire de Louis Bonaparte*, in *Œuvres*, t. IV : "Politique 1", "Bibliothèque de la Pléiade", Gallimard, Paris, 1994, p. 437-441.

Thought experiment of the third kind. An anguished puppet travels through time

In the morning, the news. The sport. France was beaten in the final. I had not even followed the match the day before, so indifferent was I to this non-event, so exasperated was I even by the omnipresence of soccer in the media, with the exception of certain newspapers on France Culture. And yet, that morning, I felt in the pit of my stomach a rather strong impression of sadness, of disappointment, which amazed me. The result of the game had been decided in the last minutes. No luck. Fate. These worn out words, these clichés of which I thought I had long since done the trick, come to mind as if in spite of myself. Of what hold, of what narrative trap am I unwittingly captive?

Spinoza, Freud, all my friends! I admit to myself, now, that I had allowed myself to be a little contaminated, captured in the horizontality of a story that had been preached everywhere: "Being French and European champions, a great family, fraternity, we are the best, etc." In the street, the day before, I had passed a group of supporters; one of them had called out to me in a tone of joyful complicity that had annoyed me. And I would have been fooled all the same? Emotional mimicry? Strange!

Let's associate. As if it were a dream. Vertically. Childhood. A prize, a first place, missed at school. Serious, but not brilliant like others. My image at stake. My parents in disappointed expectation. So, while other things slowly come up, little by little my gloom fades away. And, rather surprisingly, I *find*, with regard to what had affected me, a serene indifference.

To deliver our frail and singular little music from the sad passions induced by certain encounters, a thought of the third kind would be to invent. Both operative and associative, it should be deployed in two directions. To give place to two awarenesses. An approach that seems difficult, if not impossible, as it goes beyond the traditional academic divisions. Can we simultaneously apprehend a social reality that is *unknown* even though we are immersed in it *and* an individual history punctuated by emotions whose origin is most often *unconscious*? How can we not lose Bourdieu when we read Freud or when we are on a couch, how can we not forget Freud when we investigate the misery of the world? One thinks here of the illusionist who explains a trick to the spectators while hiding a second one from them.

It is the representation that we have of ourselves that *unknowingly* crystallizes this double secret. That of our "self", the more or less gratifying role that a group such as a theater group has insidiously assigned to us. *And*, invisible vertical, the presence of our past. *Secret histories, in a way perpendicular*, as are, on a musical score, a melody and its harmony. What path to adopt to face this cunning dialectic between value and meaning, Balzac and Proust[120]?

---

120. Proust in fact goes further. As if repeating Marx's own analysis of the form "value", he writes: "Since no mathematics allows us to convert Mme d'Arpajon and Mme de Montpensier into homogeneous quantities, it would have been impossible for me to answer if I had been asked which one seemed superior to the other. However, it is this absurd question which could distress the two women. See *Le Côté de Guermantes II* II in *À la recherche du temps perdu*, "Bibliothèque de la Pléiade", t. II, Gallimard, Paris, 1991, p. 858. Marx in fact, starting from his discovery - the real nature of the exchange value and the extortion of a "surplus value" - describes, as we have been reminded, the barbaric universe of the human-commodities, exploited without being aware of it. A phantasmagoria: the world in reverse of money. Our world. That of economic exchange but also of debt, we will come back to that. A rigged universe, the casino of Las Vegas where we play our lives without knowing that the dice are loaded. One of the secrets of anguish.

It would probably be necessary, first of all, to *identify the story* - it flew, it swooped down on us like a Hitchcock bird - where our image was imprisoned. To perceive its conventional character. To flush out the words which, we feel anxiously, try to imprison us, are capable of killing us. These words which however assign stereotyped roles ("I am the girl who always disappoints") in a play full of commonplaces ("to succeed in life"). A bad comedy, in short, that it is not easy to unmask because its clichés, when they are stuck to us, are always already *caught* in stories dating back to childhood, thus invested with the first affects. The form that the mythology of a family had to take one day so that we incorporate the opinions, the apparent logic. The deceptive knowledge of the first kind denounced by Spinoza. Now, the essential characteristic of the affects is that they do not obey to a *logical causality* but to an *associative causality*. We can indeed, by associating, find the past where an affect had its source. *A past, unbeknownst to us, mounted.*

The second step of the process consists therefore in identifying the montage which, starting from an old image of ourselves - a guilt-ridden child, a submissive schoolboy -, gives a semblance of reality to the simplistic but anguishing narrative of which we are prisoners. Incarcerated in the logical causality, the thread of this narrative, we thought we were freely thinking, "feeling", and we angrily realize that we were "spoken", "acted", like an anguished puppet unaware of the strings that activate it. The deceptive entanglement of a social role and an arrangement of our emotional past.

The anguish, of the past disguised in future, we said. To become aware of the fact that one is captive of a montage, is to be already almost delivered from a false destiny. "To have broken bones in one's head", as Sartre explained to his leftist friends after May 68 who did not understand that by writing his Flaubert, he was pursuing a kind of self-analysis, while going the same day to militate at Renault[121]. Reinventing "the family idiot", he was not going back "the course of time", he was modifying his own past by taking it apart.

Because associative causality does not content itself, defying science fiction, with questioning the irreversibility of *time*. It renders the very concept

---

121. Philippe GAVI, Jean-Paul SARTRE, Pierre VICTOR [Benni Lévi], *On a raison de se révolter*, Gallimard, Paris, 1974, p. 70-83 and p. 104-106.

of time useless. Indeed, there is no longer any need for "time" to ensure a continuity between moments, the affect - faster in a way than light - takes care of it. The affect, substance of the lived, carrier of *sense* and yet so long put aside of any speculative step. It is moreover precisely this denial of the affect that hinders a real philosophical apprehension of "time". This in spite of certain approaches - that of Kant[122], that of Bergson[123] - where, one feels it well, something desperately tries to express itself. Fortunately, music provides for it, indispensable, essential. Bachelard had understood it[124].

---

122. "Time is nothing other than the form of internal sense, that is, of the intuition of ourselves and of our inner state", Immanuel KANT, *Critique of Pure Reason, Philosophical Works*, t. I: "From the first writings to the *Critique of Pure Reason* (1747-1781)", "Bibliothèque de la Pléiade", Gallimard, Paris, 1980, p. 794

123. "For if, by chance, the moments of real duration, glimpsed by an attentive consciousness, penetrated each other instead of being juxtaposed [...]", Henri BERGSON, *Essai sur les données immédiates de la conscience* (1898), Éditions Skira, Genève, 1945 p. 180.

124. "On the musical level, for example, we will have to show that what makes the *continuity*, it is always an obscure dialectic which calls *feelings* about impressions, *memories* about sensations [...] sentimental reconstructions which agglomerate beyond the

But there is another way to pierce the double secret of an affect. To pass by the dream, this unusual nocturnal history which makes us live so astonishing ruptures with the usual accounts. The inventive strangeness of the dream, thus, is opposed to the stereotype of the reveries. From this perspective, the struggle of dreams is the climax of the struggle of narratives. A dream can break a *narrative identity* which distresses or depresses by substituting an improbable singularity - ours - reopening to the imaginary all the possibilities[125]. To feel lost, for example, in a forgotten city, to seek one's way. And to wake up. To associate on its dream then, it is to give itself a chance to find this way. To change mood. And to make thus of this dream *an event.*

---

real sensation thanks to the blur and the torpor of the emotion, thanks to the confused mixture of memories and hopes [...]", Gaston BACHELARD, *La dialectique de la durée*, PUF, Paris, 2001, p. 113, repr. "Quadrige", PUF, Paris, 2013 (my italics).
125. It is perhaps a failure of this dream function that explains the bizarre and much-discussed "multiple personality" syndrome observed in the United States and the Netherlands between 1980 and 1990. In this pathology, everything happens as if the patients had been forced to invent a multiplicity of characters, most often stereotyped: "a 50 year old man", "brutal and thief", then "sympathetic and hard-working", "a 5 year old girl"...

It can even happen that the "dream worker", this mysterious unconscious creator, summons several narrators. This is the case in *The Injection Made to Irma*, the dream where Freud, through his associations, finds the origin of a feeling of guilt and calls upon his true friend, "Dr. M***", as a lawyer against the prosecutor "Otto"[126]. A dreamlike court where two opposing views of the same case confront each other.

The most surprising thing is the little interest that those who anxiously watch for possible messages from hypothetical extraterrestrial creatures take in their dreams. Where does the composer of the dream go to look for his materials? "In" the virtual universe proper to each being: its memory. On the other side of the dream.

IV. Memory, a pluriverse

"The thing may seem strange: while Freud did not elaborate a theory of memory, if one understands by theory an overall construction aiming at synthesis, one

---

126. Sigmund FREUD, *The Interpretation of Dreams, op. cit.* pp. 255-256.

can say that all his writings deal only with memory or rather with memories."

J.-B. Pontalis, Preface to Sigmund Freud, *Eight studies on memory and its disorders.*

Diurnal holes and black remains. Insistence of the affect

"A man possesses himself in flashes. And even when he possesses himself, he does not quite reach himself."
Antonin Artaud.

One finds oneself, one morning, facing the dream of the night. An unedited story, unbelievable, offered if one decides to do so, to all the associations of which a memory is capable. *Mnèmosunè*, this memory of which the Greeks made a divinity. The virtual set of all the possible assemblies.

What, without much effort, is quickly found: some details of the day before the dream. The *diurnal remains*. In the course of a day, indeed, at the chance of encounters, we sometimes felt inexplicably touched by a word, a gesture, a mimic. A light, fleeting wound, as if, in the false light of day, the operating thought had not given an affect time to really express itself. Small scratch quickly forgotten, starting point however for the "work of the dream[127]". Crucial relay, this diurnal remainder is however, curiously, one of the Freudian concepts of which one speaks the least.

Let us risk a metaphor. The "diurnal remainder" could be, in the course of the encounters, the trace left in the conscience *by the secret blooming of a reminiscence*, just as a "black hole" is dug in the cosmos after the explosion of a star[128]. At the same time *diurnal hole and black remainder*, the diurnal remainder would be then, through the latent affective energy of its condensations, a possible opening towards former explosions, supernovae of the childhood. The scenes of our distant past that, in the pluriverse of the memory, an affect had brought closer[129].

———————————

127. Freud, on the subject of "dream work": "The difference between these two forms of thought is a difference of nature, which is why they cannot be compared. Dream work does not think or calculate; in a more general way, *it does not judge*; it is satisfied with transforming" in *L'interprétation des rêves, op. cit.* p. 432 (my emphasis).
128. Jean-Pierre Luminet, *L'enfant qui voulait voir l'invisible*, "Circo", Gallimard/CNRS, Paris, 2007. See also: http://www. dailymotion.com/relevance/search/luminet/video/xlybo4_ luminet-partie-1_tech
129. "Plurivers", the word is from Jean-Clet Martin, *Plurivers*.

Triumph of the affect. The astonishing feeling of "lived" that gives the dream loses then of its mystery: an affect come from far had made *alive* the strangest oniric narrative creations because it *is*, although most often unavowed, the very substance of the lived. The affects, shapeless and promising, marvelous clouds, would be thus more essential than the representations. And even that the concepts. These affects which appear such the lightning of a murderous resonance between the glance of another and a childhood, irremediable disease which interminably flows according to its slope. Between the two - a look and a childhood -, an intermediary unfortunately essential to the first sightings of the other, a simple cliché, sometimes, which however can hurt. *The stereotypes are indeed most often inhabited by the core of an old pain that they went to recover to give themselves a semblance of life.* It is this pain, temporarily appeased, that a seemingly banal word, a look, is enough to awaken. Because the pictures are undermined by this ancient affect, like seemingly harmless, innocent playgrounds, which would conceal in their basement grenades from the First World War, frighteningly rusty, but always ready to explode.

Essai sur la fin du monde, PUF, Paris, 2010.

5. Listening/dreaming. Therapeutic track

Faced with the apparently incomprehensible dreamlike montage that challenges it, memory can thus be a war machine launched forward by the desire to understand. *A machine to understand.* It sniffs then the dream, as to discover there the hidden explosives that it conceals, then it shreds it, morcelle, *dismounts* it. The time and the space bitten, undone by the free association, the monster-memory, this unimaginable singularity is going from then on to *assimilate* one by one what remained of the dream: potentially gigantic crumbs. The meaning of the dream enters the past and suddenly illuminates it, unfolds it. It can then, as if it had the force to tear off a planet from its orbit, make a being come out of a history in which he was unknowingly stuck, the secret rhyme, always the same, unconscious source of his anxious anticipations.

"Yesterday you intimidated me. You are now, this morning, but one of my diurnal remains." By associating, the dreamer has regained *his* gaze. Freed from evil gravitations, his past is now ready for new adventures.

In the *assemblies of memory, the shortest "path" between two associated representations would be the affect that is common to them*[130]. That an affect can be a path is, it is true, difficult to conceive, so much so that affectivity is usually relegated outside the objects of knowledge proper. Except by Spinoza.

Affective geometry of memory : Einstein slips between Spinoza and Freud

> "Riemann is thus, in the history of mathematics, a strange magician [...] a kind of barbarian whose reflection will be taken seriously only by Einstein, renewing his vision of space [...]"
>
> Jean-Clet Martin, *Hell of philosophy*.

When Spinoza writes that nobody, to his knowledge, has determined the nature and force of affects, nor defined the control that the mind can exercise over them, affects that must be treated as lines, planes or bodies[131], he obviously cannot foresee that at the beginning of the 20th century a physicist, a

---

130. It is not *the affect* that would move from one representation to another, but the representations that would slide on the rail of the same affect during the interpretation of a dream, for example. The affect is by this strictly conform to the definition of a *structure*: invariant relation between interchangeable elements.
131. Baruch SPINOZA, *Ethics*, III, preface.

Spinozian as it were, would upset this same geometry that, metaphorically, he invoked. And that beyond this upheaval, a third attribute (besides extent and reasoning thought) - associative thought - would be invented, allowing us to better understand the very essence of affect: the form in which *the sensitivity of a memory* is expressed.

Much could be said about the depression of mathematical innovators. It has already been said about Cantor. Concerning Gauss, Riemann and other inventors of non-Euclidean geometries, this *no* to Euclid could be a key. That of an ancient refusal. The raging "No!" of a child to the prohibitions of training: "Don't dream! Stand up straight!" As if these depressed creators had felt that a ban from the past could be hidden behind their melancholy[132].

To find a forgotten dimension in order to tear themselves away from the montages in which they

---

132. "In an experiment that has become classic, Zeigarnik (1927) shows *that unfinished actions are better remembered than completed ones*. The adult's "No!" prohibits the child from performing the action he was undertaking. As a result, the increasing number of prohibitions leaves in its wake a corresponding number of unfinished tasks. Their common element, the "No" [...]", René Arped Spitz, *Le Non et le Oui*, PUF, Paris, 1962, p. 34-35.

felt caught, to change space in order to change their mood, this is perhaps what, more or less consciously, these slightly sad mathematicians were looking for. At the same time, they returned to certain childhood ways of thinking, abandoning "the shortest paths" in favor of wandering along the side paths, the aimless curves.

In Newton's time, two parallel lines never met. Not allowed. Euclid. Escaping from a space sealed by Kant, Riemann, one day, said *no to* Euclid and placed the parallels on a sphere. Curved, becoming meridians[133], they now meet at one pole of the sphere. As a result, Riemann provided Einstein with the mathematical model he was lacking.

Einstein, then, bent space-time backwards. A compass shown to him by his father when he was 4 years old may have been the *transerelle*[134] that led

---

133. "Geodesics": the shortest path from one point to another.
134. See Max DORRA, *Lutte des rêves et interprétation des classes. Dismantling a trick of illusion, op. cit.* p. 145: the word *transerelle* is a neologism that I have proposed, which means "bridge of transgression". An apparently harmless object or word that inexplicably makes one dream or even, on occasion, change one's mood. It is in reality the replica of the object or word that, unconsciously, like a body floating in the eye, we carry in our memory: the common element to disappeared scenes

5. Listening/dreaming. Therapeutic track

him to explode the reductive set-up imprisoning physicists since Newton. Formidable transgression[135].

Einstein can now *interpret* the universe: it is the matter which, by bending the space, digs there the very furrows where necessarily it flows. Law of structure. After this interpretation, the Earth turning

---

of the past, the thread that connected them, in short, what remains when we have forgotten everything. These memories can sometimes be recovered - with all their emotional charge - if, starting from transerelles, we let associations and metaphors go. The transerelles are thus vehicles thanks to which, by exploring one's own memory, one has a chance to find a lost meaning. As bridges of transgression, they can give access, if one is not too afraid, to "forbidden districts" of the memory. Examples of transgressions: trimethylamine in Freud's dream; madeleine, a badly squared paving stone, a small yellow wall, in Proust; perfume of the lady in black, in Gaston Leroux.

135. How *transgressive* were the non-Euclidean geometries that managed to *get out of* Euclid's Elements, the archetype of the axiomatized theory. This theory had fascinated philosophers and mathematicians for two thousand years, notably Gauss, a precursor in non-Euclidean geometry, but *who had not dared to publish his work*. To be compared with the advice of caution that Paul Langevin had received, from Jean Perrin in particular, concerning his work of 1905-1906, which was close to that of Einstein: see Michel BIEZUNSKI, *Einstein à Paris*, Presses universitaires de Vincennes, Saint-Denis, 1991, p. 130.

around the Sun does nothing more than slide in the gullies of space.

What about memory? These are the real laws of structure of this virtual universe, governing a kind of "gravitation" of the past, which *enter into crisis at the* moment when the other appears, when his eye becomes a look. A look that assigns us a certain image of ourselves. Everything happens indeed as if, in front of *the other,* this image had, like a star in the Einsteinian space-time, the curious power to change the structure, the affective geometry of our memory. To bend it in its own way, to reorganize it *to the point of creating new convergences* ready to trap in their assembly any new representation.

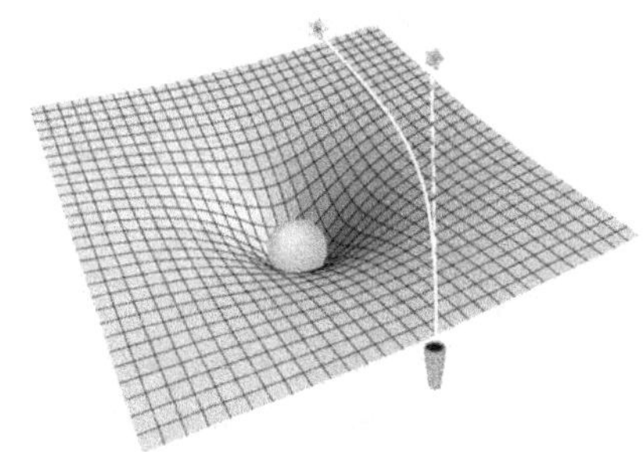

5. Listening/dreaming. Therapeutic track

It is indeed towards this image of ourselves that all our associations converge when we are taken in such a montage. Image that has been imposed to us by the other and that this convergence, precisely, accredits. All the more so as it is likely to reactivate old associative paths, latent until then.

Because this pole, this representation has a history. It is indeed from an image of ourselves, a long time ago, that everything had begun: the stammerings of affectivity, the acquisition of the first words, the emergence of the first structures. It is thus not surprising that, making us go backwards a certain way, this "identity" which comes to us from the others can wake up this *old assembly*. And to make us find again our fear in front of the box of labels where we were going to lock up.

Curvature of memory, curvature of universe

"It is possible that spatiality is the projection of the extension of the psychic apparatus. Presumably no other derivation. Instead of the *a priori* conditions of the psychic apparatus according to Kant. Psyche is extended, knows nothing about it."

Sigmund Freud, *Results, Ideas, Problems*, June 1938.

"Memory is not a machine. It is a 'psychic being' and perhaps even our *psychic being*."

J.-B. Pontalis, Preface to Sigmund Freud, *Eight studies on memory and its disorders*.

The *memory*, our "psychic being". Indeed, everything happens as if the past always saturated the air before each perception. Nothing to do with Plato's cave. Here, it is the war. The sensation, when it arises, is immediately assailed by an invisible army of ghosts. How can we imagine this great shadow, the past, which desperately seeks a future with the complicity of the present? The whole past *is there*, masked, ready to pounce. All there, with its unfinished gestures, its sketched variations, in short an impatient trampling at the door of any perception. A twig, a stain on the wall, a look, it is enough to linger a little on anything that arouses even fleetingly an affect to feel that a memory is measuring itself against the present. The conscious perception is ultimately only what remains of these confrontations.

Then come the questions suggested by Freud's statement, quoted at the beginning of this chapter.

But in order to answer this question, it is necessary to agree on precise definitions. Spinoza's definitions

5. Listening/dreaming. Therapeutic track

will be adopted here. If "the mind is the idea of the body", as he says, then there is no need for Kantian *a priori* forms or "transcendental". The Euclidean space proves to be, not an *a priori*, but a form *imposed* by the very structure of the sensory apparatus essential to locate itself there, apparatus organized - it cannot be a chance - precisely *according to its three dimensions*. It is, as we know, the semicircular canals of the inner ear[136].

---

136. Bone tubes containing a liquid which, by inertia, moves in the opposite direction of the body's movements. This liquid thus exerts a pressure on the internal wall of these semicircular canals whose *arrangement, in the three dimensions of space,* allows a precise tracking of these movements. Incredible as it may seem, the details of this process are envisaged by Spinoza who, in all likelihood, was unaware of the existence of the semicircular canals; see *Ethics*, II, postulate V: "When a fluid part of the human body is determined by an external body to strike a soft part often, it changes its surface and imprints on it, so to speak, certain traces of the external body which pushes it."

It is surprising that, apart from Henri Poincaré, this questioning has never been proposed. It is strange to *forget the human body*. This body that Fallope had nevertheless opened to dissect its auditory apparatus. He had thus been able to describe as early as 1561, two hundred years before the *Critique of Pure Reason*, these orthogonal channels on which the control of our balance depends. The *vertigo*, which deconstructs space, is generated by the disturbance of this sensory apparatus.

There is in the same way, as astonishing, a real oblivion of *the memory*, this virtual being which can be as painful as a body, the actual being[137]. And it is precisely an affect which ensures the continuity between virtual and actual. When we associate, leaving "the shortest way", the straight certainties of the operative thought, we let thus little by little return our past. The spirit is entirely then, without that it is necessarily conscious of it, *an idea of that memory*. Of its veins, of its associative curves. "Curves", this same word which comes from time to time under the pen

---

137. Memory inseparable from the body, recalls Spinoza, *Ethics*, II, proposition 18, scholia. It is under this angle that he evokes the amnesia of a Spanish poet. *Ethics*, IV, proposition 39, scolie.

of Kierkegaard ("one curves the eternity in the time by imagination[138]") of Bergson ("our curvature of original soul[139]"), of Proust, when they speak about the memory.

Vulnerable curves indeed because they depend on the montage where they are taken. Two beings face to face have thus difficulty to understand why, eyes in eyes, they sometimes feel a certain uneasiness at the moment when the eye of the other became a glance. The fact is that *one cannot simultaneously apprehend the gaze of the other and perceive his eyes*[140]. At the precise moment when the eye of the other becomes a glance on us, the space does not curl in the strict sense, it metamorphoses. In the same way that a vertigo signals a lesion of the apparatus of the balance, this uneasiness indicates that a whole memory, the organization even of its curvatures, its assembly, were modified.

A geometry of affectivity then takes shape, the same one perhaps that Spinoza evoked. The gaze of

---

138. Sören KIERKEGAARD, *The Concept of Anguish*, "Ideas", Gallimard, Paris, 1969, p. 154.
139. Henri BERGSON, *L'évolution créatrice*, Éditions Skira, Genève, 1945, p. 23.
140. Jean-Paul SARTRE, *Being and Nothingness* (1943), Gallimard, 1971, p. 316.

the other, when it arises, is indeed *both* immediate presence and impassable distance, as if this very presence, paradoxically, deployed a distance that inexplicably keeps us apart[141]. However, this passage of the eye to the glance does not cross anything. Nothing but a being. A being, *touched* indeed, whose body stiffens at this moment, as if reached in its heart. In reality to its memory. Sartre, one of the few to have attempted to describe this moment, speaks of shame. Shame, a child slapped because he was dirty. To think this passage from the eye to the glance by *linking* associations and conceptualizations (the knowledge of the third kind), it is to give ourselves a chance perhaps to *better control,* one day, the formidable geometry of our own affectivity. And thus to return to a memory all its possibilities.

The story of a reversal: the metaphor that hid its game

To give back its possibilities to a memory is to recover disappeared modes of perception. To change the world. Then, the church of Auvers can tear itself away from its clichés. The terrace of a café flies

---

141. *Id.* at *Ibid.*

away in the night. The trembling of the outline in Van Gogh's work, the stridency of the colors, this is it. A breach in the memories-screens. The precise, seizing instant of a takeoff. To take off, to give back its availability to the memory, its *possible* future to the past. To allow again *to listen to* all its history, to all its potential histories[142].

The metaphor, too, when it is born of a wild *association*, has its own movement, its force of tearing away. It too, carrying beyond words, pulls out of language. Unforgettable link, purely personal, between two representations, singular curvature, untimely way towards the knowledge of the third kind.

To speak metaphorically of "curvature" in relation to memory, the virtual source of all metaphors, is to give a sense, in a way fractal, to this part of a whole. What is a metaphor indeed? The *emergence of*

---

142. "Travelling is very useful, it makes the imagination work. All the rest is only disappointments and tiredness. Our journey is entirely imaginary. That is its strength. It goes from life to death. Men, beasts, cities and things, everything is imagined. It is a novel, nothing but a fictional story. Littré says it, who is never wrong. And first of all everyone can do the same. It is enough to close the eyes. It is on the other side of life", Louis-Ferdinand Céline, exergue of *Journey to the End of the Night*.

an associative thought tearing itself away from the rectilinear logic of the operative thought.

Freud, in his enigmatic sentence, speaks about "projection". The projection of a volume makes it lose a dimension. A sphere is reduced to a circle. To return the metaphor of the curvature, it is to find its lost dimension[143]. Its history, its transgressive birth. Its memory, precisely. This metaphor thus hid its game. Revisited, turned upside down in a way, it is not satisfied anymore to *figure* a memory. As if, in certain cases, whereas the abstract language speaks only in the figurative, it is the metaphor which, producing a concrete sensation, would speak in the proper[144]. Like a dream, it had a latent content. Freely associate, then, becomes, in act, *a movement found* which, at every moment, must tear itself away from the tangent of the codes to persevere in its curve, its always threatened singularity. To resist to the operative thought.

___

143. Let's recall Eisenstein's project to write "a spherical book".
144. Henri BERGSON, *La pensée et le mouvant, op. cit.*

5. Listening/dreaming. Therapeutic track

Thus, we believed to exist whereas we were only the characters of a story which one had told us. For we live, most often, only on the tangent of ourselves. To leave a story or a geometry, as Bernhard Riemann dared, is to be able to invent the possible again[145]. Two parallels never meet? Let's change geometry: they can now meet each other, and have fun with each other in the dream. Who would have said that one night Swann and... Napoleon III would meet in a dream, for better or for worse, and that Swann would then change his mood, that is to say, his emotional universe?

To bring together an association which springs up and a curvature freeing itself from its tangent is not indeed, as we have seen, only a figure of speech. A metaphor produces meaning because it comes from the very being. This is why *the meaning of a metaphor*, its impulse, can make words *dance*, deliver a body by making it hear again the melodic curves of a memory.

---

145. Lewin: "The curved space of which the modern science makes so much case can constitute itself a very early experience of the life of the individual, an experience fallen in the lapse of memory under the influence of the later Euclidian perceptions", quoted *in* SAMI-ALI, *The imaginary space*, "Knowledge of the unconscious", Gallimard, Paris, 1974, p. 135.

And this impulse can even be contagious to the point of freeing in the other a way for its own metaphors. Thus we find, no doubt, the curvilinear forms that invariably seem to reveal the first drawings of all the children of the world[146]... *Because the memory is curved but it does not know it.*

Freud's surprising statement was therefore not as paradoxical as it might seem. Perhaps it even opened up new avenues.

"Strange quark", "Wormhole", "White fountain", "Death of a star", "Black hole": aren't these metaphors associations that came to the mind of a researcher one day, before being mathematized? Not to mention the "initial singularity" of the Big Bang where Hawking joins Artaud. Denied in the name of "scientific objectivity", the affectivity of a being, its reminiscences are always, however, surprisingly present.

This is obvious in the particular case of *magnetism,* its "attractions", its "magnets". One might wonder whether the very concept of magnetic field, this troubling entity, is not the projection of something else. Another "field"?

---

146. V. and O. Marc, *Premiers dessins d'enfants. Les tracés de la mémoire*, Nathan, Paris, 2002.

5. Listening/dreaming. Therapeutic track

We are anguished grains of filings. The field of debt and guilt

> "But what is a life if you don't tell it to yourself? And, as we know, for one life, there are a hundred possible biographies."
>
> J.-B. Pontalis, *L'amour des commencements.*

Faced with a magnet, a grain of filings, if it were endowed with consciousness, would be stunned to discover that what *affected it*, to the point of assigning it a place among the other grains, was not an "inner disease", nor a mysterious power coming from the magnet and acting at a distance, but an invisible *line of force* in a *magnetic field*[147]. The ontological vertigo of a small piece of iron unaware of the magnetic field in which it is immersed[148].

---

147. The revolutionary concept of "field", advanced against Newton by Faraday - apprentice bookbinder, self-taught physicist -, will be thereafter a privileged source of metaphors. For Bourdieu in particular, who evoked economic, political and cultural "fields", "each field having its own logic".

148. A field, "an autonomous reality that does not refer to anything else and that is not linked to any support", Albert EINSTEIN, *Œuvres choisies*, t. V, Éditions du Seuil/CNRS, Paris, 1992, p. 84. "The electromagnetic field in empty space is a thing possessing an autonomous physical reality, independent of any

The grain of anguished filings, it could be each of us in the *field* induced by the other. Field which reorganizes us from a certain image of ourselves, determining the lines of force of our affects[149]. Two beings sometimes believe themselves in conflict, which in reality struggle without their knowledge, each one, through the imperceptible lines of force of the narrative field which is proper to him. An agreement in love, on the contrary, it can be a connivance between "resistants", a complicity felt in front of the constraints to which each is confronted.

A word, when we are caught in its *lines of force*, assigns us, let us repeat, at the same time as a place, a certain representation of ourselves. In Nazi Germany, Victor Klemperer tells us, "language not only thinks for me, it *also directs my feelings*, it governs my entire moral being[150] [...]" An invisible theater stage

---

substance", Max von Laue *in* Françoise BALIBAR, *Einstein 1905. De l'éther aux quanta*, PUF, Paris, 1992, p. 120.

149. "The ardently realistic physicist will like to see, in the fields of force, regions of space where reigns an *affective tension*", Gaston BACHELARD, *The rationalist activity of the contemporary physics*, PUF, Paris, 1965, p. 59.

150. Victor KLEMPERER, *LTI, la langue du 3ᵉ Reich*, Albin Michel, Paris, 2003, p. 40.

5. Listening/dreaming. Therapeutic track

thus unfolds, where we are captive of a role[151]. Of a narrative identity. This is how Hitler arrived one day, telling a different story from the one that the Germans had heard and lived until then, humiliated and *made to feel guilty* by the Treaty of Versailles. And the massive *debt* it implied. If so many Germans ignored the horror of National Socialism for so long, it was largely because it offered them a new narrative and a new role in which they rediscovered a lost pride.

Debt, a seemingly banal economic notion, is in reality a real existential commitment. *Schuld*, the German word, means both "debt" and "fault": it says everything about the link between debt and guilt. Nietzsche had well noted the objective-subjective

---

151. Philip Zimbardo set up an experiment at Stanford University in 1971: volunteers were put in the shoes of prisoners and guards. The sadism used by certain "guards" was noted, as well as the corresponding depression and passivity of the "prisoners". Zimbardo concludes that *the situation provokes the behavior of the participants much more than their individual personalities*. In this sense, the results of the experiment corroborate those of the famous Milgram experiment, in which ordinary people administered to an accomplice of the experimenters and on the orders of a teacher what were presented to them as dangerous electric shocks.

nature of debt[152]. Freud, too, had spotted it during the analysis of "The Rat Man". It is that the debt, invisibly immersed in the religious field, is linked to a guilt: the history notably of the "original sin" and of the first insubordination, source of an insolvent debt. However, there is a way to free oneself from these tales: to interpret them as bad dreams[153]. By associating. For it is *affects* from childhood that *make up* the character of the "debtor". A being who lives as a subjective fatality the fallacious destiny that the objective assembly of the debt insidiously assigns to him. The relationship between a debtor and a creditor illustrates, in a certain way, *the very essence of power: the capacity to distress by setting up a memory.*

---

152. In *Genealogy of Morals*: "The essential moral concept of 'fault' has its origin in the very material idea of debt." Nietzsche insists on the fact that the debtor sometimes pledges his freedom, his body, even his life. This idea is taken up by Gilles DELEUZE and Félix GUATTARI in *Capitalisme et schizophrénie 1. L'Anti-Œdipe*, "Critique", Minuit, Paris, 1972, as well as Maurizio LAZZARATO in *La fabrique de l'homme endetté. Essay on the neoliberal condition*, Éditions Amsterdam, Paris, 2011.
153. Spinoza, in the preface to *Theological and Political Authority*, notes that in the Bible, it is often in a dream that God addresses a prophet, for example Ex. 25:22, Ge. 20:6: "In a dream he heard God say to him [...]"

As soon as one borrows, in fact, one enters into subordination. This is the case, for example, with loans granted to "poor countries" who are made to believe that they "live beyond their means". Any debt can thus incarcerate beings in the set-up induced by a guilt-inducing gaze.

In the dreams of Descartes and Freud, in the autobiographical notes of Einstein, a strange guilt

"Newton, *forgive me*. You have found all that was possible in your time for a man of the most powerful intelligence and creativity. Although we now know that if we are to attempt to have a deeper understanding of the relations of things to each other, we must replace them with ideas more remote from immediate experience, the ideas of which you were the author still dominate our thinking about physics."

Albert Einstein, *Autobiographical Notes*[154].

Stories, above all that of guilt - present since the first dream interpreted by Freud - insidiously surround us,

---

154. Banesh HOFFMANN (with the collaboration of Helen DUKAS), *Albert Einstein créateur et rebelle*, "Points Sciences", Éditions du Seuil, 1975, Paris, p. 267.

haunt us. Pirandello described characters in search of an author. We could evoke here *stories waiting for characters*. From these stereotypes, myths ensuring the cohesion of the groups, the fantasies of the individuals will feed. Stories in which we are, without our knowledge, from morning to night plunged and to which, strangely, we find it very difficult to resist. This is why "we are automatons in three quarters of our actions" as Leibniz said.

We are indeed, from childhood, taken hostage by words. That we become aware of this is not enough to free us from it. When Descartes writes "I think, therefore [...]", he is already, by this *therefore*, captive of a syllogism, in the straight line of an operative thought. "I will use, please, here freely the words of the School", will say this passionate man, lowering for a moment the mask[155]. He can then only ignore, while he believes himself free, the real nature of this *I*: the identity of the logician[156] that he borrows to

---

155. René DESCARTES, *Discours de la méthode* in *Œuvres et lettres*, "Bibliothèque de la Pléiade", Gallimard, Paris, 1966, p. 149.
156. "For logic, its syllogisms and most of its other instructions serve rather to explain to others the things one knows [...]", René DESCARTES, *Discourse on Method* in *Œuvres et lettres*, *op. cit.*, p. 136-137.

convince philosophers. Being no more, without his knowledge, than a fragment in the field of their discourse, *I*, from then on, *is thought*. One can thus imagine that his conclusive *I am* is more linked to an underlying associative thought than to a logical certainty. "I insensibly mix my daydreams with my night dreams". Playing on the word, Descartes superimposes the meaning of *meditation* on that of *dream*. He slips from one to the other as from sleep to wakefulness[157]. This, notes Christian Doumet, had been evident twenty years earlier when, emerging from three consecutive dreams, he had interpreted them. Let us note, moreover, that he had found there, according to Baillet's account, "the remorse of his conscience concerning *the sins he might have committed* during the course of his past life, which might not have been as innocent before God as before men.

This was in 1619. Three hundred years, curiously enough, before a solar eclipse allowed decisive observations in astrophysics: the light rays emitted by a

---

157. Christian DOUMET, *La déraison poétique des philosophes*, "l'autre pensée", Stock, Paris, 2010, p. 121. On Descartes' relation to dreams, the author's commentary should be read: *ibid.* p. 136-145.

star do not propagate in a straight line but follow the curvature of space in the vicinity of the sun. Einstein's theory, born from a quasi dreamlike thought experiment - moving at the speed of light -, breaking with Newton's theory ("forgive me"...), was verified. Riemann had won. And Mozart.

The music hears

"For Spinoza, the psychic and the physical are but different phenomenal forms, governed by the same laws, of a single reality."

Albert Einstein, "Letter to the Spinoza Society of America".

"This is the highest music in the order of thought," Einstein exclaimed after reading an article by the physicist Niels Bohr[158]. And regarding his own work: "The discovery of special relativity came to me by *intuition*, and *music was the driving force* behind this intuition. My discovery is the result of musical perception[159]."

---

158. Quoted by Georges DIDI-HUBERMAN, *Quand les images prennent position*, "Paradox", Minuit, Paris, 2009, p. 216.
159. http://www.solidariteetprogres.org/documents-de-fond-7/culture/la-musique-secret-du-genie-d-einstein.html

5. Listening/dreaming. Therapeutic track

Einstein delivers here a precious key. Newtonian physics, Euclidean, allowed only an imperfect theory of gravitation. It was necessary for Einstein, thanks to Riemann's geometry, to create a new physics in order to solve the problems left unresolved by Newton. Now, music is to language what Riemannian geometry is to Euclidean geometry: it goes further than the verb, even poetic, which is insufficient when it comes to expressing an affect. To the discontinuous path of the words, always weighed down by codes, it substitutes the lived continuity of its melodic curves recalling the curves of the memory. A *phrasing* rather than sentences. And it is really about *curves* tearing off from a tangent as associative thought does. At each moment indeed, at each inflection, they seem to protest: "We are not that, these themes, these fragments of past works. We follow only the line of our desire [...]" A fight to persevere in the very substance of its being, it is what the music makes *hear*. Freed from the language, it can even *listen*, until the indiscretion sometimes, so much it knows how to flush out the most intimate, to pass *between* the words, and to *hear* the forgotten in the memory of a being[160]. Because it is not the culture which remains when one has forgotten everything, it is the affect. There is a "hypermnesia of the music", just as Freud spoke about "hypermnesia of the dream". Certainly, a word sometimes of all its words softly listens. But a melody, it is with its variations, its breaks, its rhythms, that it mimes for better capturing them, the quiverings of a memory. Without words, she tells him, for better or for worse, satisfied or disappointed expectations,

---

160. A little musical phrase, one day, had suddenly made a patient relive a forgotten moment, that of his first step. A leap into the unknown. A decisive *movement* towards freedom.

5. Listening/dreaming. Therapeutic track

reversals of situation, irruptions. The incompleteness, the unpredictability of the relationship to the other. It is undoubtedly by this, by the freedom of her improvisations, that she had opened to Einstein a field of possibility. The one to face the constraints which since Newton incarcerated the physicists. And to dare to bend the universe.

One can then, as Freud had suspected, make the hypothesis that space itself could be only the "projection" of something else. Something that would not only have one more dimension but would be, by essence, different. Because the physical space, its fields, it is through our invisible past that we consider it. And we *perceive* there very often only what was in the latent state in our memory. More precisely in a montage of it. A freeze of childhood.

The magnetized space of childhood, its terrors and its joys, its resignations and its refusals, its dependence, such could be the origin of a kind of common unitary field, still difficult to conceive. The "occupied" childhood, such as those years when the only choice was to be a (camouflaged) resistant, a collaborator, or, most often, to remain fearfully silent. The so-called "family secrets" are indeed mystery-sheets. The real secret of family photos is the little song that, behind the lens, a terrible look was trying to inscribe. This old tune from which one can only *deliver one's childhood*, to get it out of subjection, by daring to reinvent, in fact to find, one's own and singular music. So that a child, always present but finally relieved of guilt, free, can like Einstein stick out his tongue at all the important[161].

"Ultimate" theory and ontological pulsation

"We know nothing in pure immersion, in the in-itself, in the soil of the *too-near*. Nor will we know anything in pure abstraction, in haughty transcendence, in the sky of the *too-far*. To know, one must take a position, which supposes to move and to constantly assume the responsibility of such a movement. This movement is *approach* as much as *deviation*: approach with reserve, deviation with desire."

Georges Didi-Huberman,
When images take a stand.

---

161. Albert Einstein: "I have always had difficulty accepting authority, and here, sticking out one's tongue at a photographer who surely expects a more solemn pose, means that one *refuses to* play the game of representation, that one *refuses to* deliver an image of oneself that conforms to the rules of the genre" (my emphasis).

5. Listening/dreaming. Therapeutic track

Without doubt, a theory definitively reconciling general relativity and quantum mechanics will emerge one day in physics. We can, in an apparently different field, imagine another approach, even more liberating than those allowing to explore the cosmos. Bringing together Einstein and Freud[162], it would authorize an extraordinary adventure: the affective journey allowing us to go to the other without losing ourselves. A risky *return journey* since the other, by distressing us, can deprive us of the return ticket.

A pulsation. *To go to the other is* to accept to feel for a moment one's own memory reduced to a montage, a montage adapted to the presence of the stranger. *Without losing oneself:* to find one's singularity on the way back, a singularity that evolves if it is better and better assumed. To rediscover in this way the infinity of potential montages. Freedom.

The montage is a heartbeat, says Godard. The physical body has its own rhythms, of course, but everything happens as if it were invisibly doubled

---

162. This, Einstein had, it seems, sensed since, invited in 1932 by the League of Nations to debate the problem that would please him with a person of his choice, it was Freud whom he had chosen, inviting him to discuss with him the question: "Why war?"

by another body, Artaud's "Body without Organs" perhaps, the giant, virtual being of the memory[163]. Now, it is *the existence of* this virtual being, its singular pulsatility, which gives its *style*, its meaning to the physical body. Murch, a brilliant editor, noticed that at the moment of an exchange, the eyes sometimes blink when, interrupting the story that each one in secret was telling himself, a connection occurs which announces a new editing[164]. Our gaze then turns away for a moment from the other's gaze, the time to find ourselves again.

---

163. Which brings us back to Proust. Proust who wrote about Einstein: "We seem to have an analogous way of deforming Time. Marcel PROUST, *Lettres*, Plon, Paris, 2004, p. 1053 (letter from the night of December 9 to 10, 1921).

164. "The unconscious attention we pay to blinks seems to me to be *a hidden dimension of our daily lives as* well. The simple fact of perceiving, without being aware of it, that someone blinks too much, or not enough, or at the wrong time, can make us nervous. Indeed, we understand that this person is not really listening to us, and that his thoughts do not follow the same path as ours. Conversely, a person who is focused on what we are saying *will blink at the right time and at the right frequency.* As a result, *we will feel comfortable with them,*" Walter MURCH, *In the Blink of an Eye. Past, Present and Future of Editing, op. cit.* p. 89 (my emphasis).

5. Listening/dreaming. Therapeutic track

The other. An emotional shock shattering all theories. A moment of ontological bewilderment, before any social identification. A form, a color, never met. Movements also, gestures, a new choreography. The unknown essence of a being, its strange dissonances, its unpredictable rhythms, its unusual timbre: music seems close to it, but it does not completely account for it. It is only the metaphor of it. For it is the keyboard of our memory that is at stake here, whose every key can *affect* us, risking to reorganize us entirely. There is thus neither subject nor object, but this invisible keyboard where the other plays his life in the same time that he puts ours in suspension.

Then, face to face, without blinking, the other begins to exist. A *becoming* that, in the initial associative panic, seemed definitively impossible. Such a fulguration, that, even if we don't know it yet, we will never leave each other again. An ephemeral blaze, it will however definitively inscribe its crazy singularity. The investment of a difference. We discover that the other is capable of *inventing us*, of revealing to us notes, chords never heard among the infinity of the possible notes, chords. A new, unpredictable way - a celebration? a drama? - of *being*. This is also what so many patients are desperately looking for, without knowing it, in their interlocutor, their therapist.

Here the word is missing. Neither music, nor dance, nor image, nor film. Nor even composition of all that. Should we create a new concept in front of the other, in this vacillation? But the other refuses any philosophical apprehension. Only the Spinozian third kind of knowledge could, it seems, have been cut to its measure. To be at the height of this affect/concept/event, surprising editor of our memory. Music, even if it is the one that has ventured the furthest, is alas, like space, only a projection, the desperate attempt to *say* this unthought that has one more dimension than all the symphonies of Mozart - and Wolfgang knew it well.

It is not surprising that Einstein loved Riemann and Mozart. The former, thanks to the rebellious model he provided, offered him the example of a deliverance. The second, by its dissonances, its unpredictable melodic curves, made him feel the joy of discovery[165]. For the unitary field of reality that he

---

165. Banesh HOFFMANN (with the collaboration of Helen DUKAS), *Albert Einstein, creator and rebel, op. cit*, p. 268. Let us recall that János Bolyai, co-inventor with Gauss and Lobatchevski of the hyperbolic non-Euclidean geometry, once

5. Listening/dreaming. Therapeutic track

had sought all his life in vain in physics, was perhaps reflected there, secretly, under his fingers, long before the theory of strings had been imagined, in the very life of his violin. The dimension of *knowing/understanding* where both Riemann and Mozart had their place.

The country of the third kind.

The country of the third kind. Concerto for four pianos. Eternity and infinity

"...] this separation between past, present and future has the value of an illusion, however tenacious it may be.

Albert Einstein (March 21, 1955), one month before his death. Letter about the death of his old friend Michele Besso.

"Cause of oneself", the first words of the *Ethics*. To become again the cause of oneself. This is only possible, as we have seen, by freeing a child from the trick of illusion in which he is caught: a montage.

---

provoked thirteen hussar officers under this single reservation: to be able to play the violin as a relaxation after two consecutive duels - see Imre HERMANN, *Parallélismes*, "Freud et son temps", Denoël, Paris, 1980, p. 37.

Because, to *go back* "the time", as we have seen, there is no need for science fiction: it is enough to *dismantle* the memory. This is how we can find the child of the past. Not the ashamed child who appears in the suddenly incomprehensibly anguished adult. Not this memory-screen. No, *the child in its very being*, the one who, without really knowing it, impatiently waited. The multiplicity of possible languages before the acquisition of language. The child who does not speak yet but who already communicates, by the music of gestures and rhythms, by the miracle of the smile too, which appears and upsets.

This possibility to get out of the most subtle confinements, it is what it is necessary to try to make understand to the other *in-fans*, the former subjugated child, who anguishes, despairs the adult when he suddenly invests him, until making him *forget* - as one forgets a dream - the possibility of a deliverance however many times lived. These moments, he will be able to find them however when he will associate, precisely on a dream. "Now I *am and* I think". The "true idea", inseparable from an affect, it is what he will feel then, like Bergotte in front of the small yellow wall of the painting of Vermeer. The time and the space vanished. When the "infinite" of Spinoza

5. Listening/dreaming. Therapeutic track

is discovered, so difficult to really understand, this eternity of a beginning.

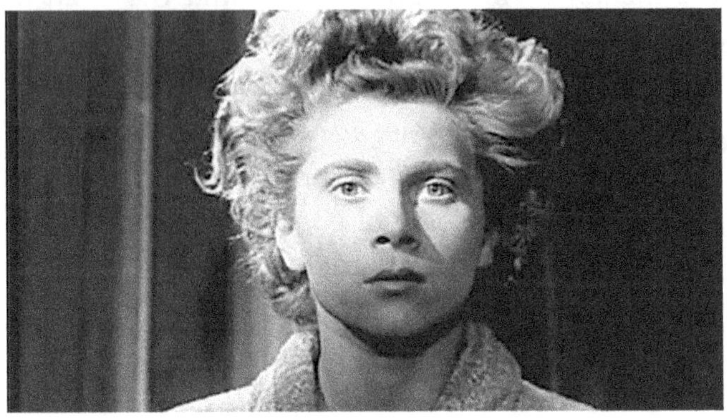

This is undoubtedly what emerges from certain shots of a film when they are accompanied by music that makes the montage waver. Bach's *Concerto for Four Pianos*, for example, bursting forth, illuminating in their inexorable cruelty, the last shots of Les *Enfants terribles*, Melville's film (from a script by Cocteau). The image of Elisabeth, played by Nicole Stéphane, that we find again in a surprising way, for a brief moment, forever, in Godard's film *Farewell to Language*. The face of a rebel.

The true third dimension in cinema, the one that gives access to the knowledge of the third kind, is sometimes born from the music of a film. A music that makes the images dream. Like a dream, moreover, it is very quickly forgotten. "Music works best, in my opinion, when it channels an emotion already created from the story line and the film[166]." It is as if the music has been watching, listening - and *hearing* - a hidden dimension, which it reveals, or rather always seems to be about to *reveal.* The heart then beats faster. "There was not a breath of wind, and that night the music had spread throughout the black ship, like an injunction from heaven, like a command from God, the content of which was unknown. She had cried because she had thought of that man from Cholon, her lover, and she had not been sure all of a sudden that she had not loved him, *a love that she had not seen* because it had been lost in history like water in the sand and *that she was only finding it now*, at this moment of music thrown across the sea[167]."

In the country of the third kind, we no longer forget the essentials. Anguish face to face, for example. This is what Daniel Barenboim, as a fervent Spinozian, was

---

166. Michael ONDAATJE, *Conversations with Walter Murch*, *op. cit.* p. 185.
167. Marguerite DURAS, *The Lover*, Minuit, Paris, 1992.

undoubtedly trying to answer with his West-Eastern Divan Orchestra, composed of Palestinians, Israelis, Egyptians, Jordanians, Turks, Lebanese, Syrians and Iranians[168]. Through the rhythms, the "music" of the other, one can indeed from time to time "enter" in a way into his memory, try to understand him.

Unexpected mimics, unexpected gestures, body rhythms attest to the singularity of an individual. It is by creating resonances that a melody insinuates itself in a being. Spinoza: "Bodies are distinguished from each other by motion and rest, speed and slowness, and not by substance[169]." Spinoza, our teacher to all, writes Debussy[170].

This unknown language, ours, we keep forgetting and the music, even if it is only a distant whisper, keeps reminding us. The language of a life where there are only beginnings.

To find again these crystals of meaning, this freedom, is to deliver oneself from an anguish from

---

168. https://www.youtube.com/watch?v=tp-EWGRGK7Q#t=119; https://www.youtube.com/watch?v=-8Ovg1v7F98
169. Baruch SPINOZA, *Ethics*, II, Lemma 1.
170. "Letter to Ernest Chausson", 5 June 1893, *in* Claude DEBUSSY, *Correspondance (1872-1918)*, Gallimard, Paris, 2005, p. 135.

which all the powers profit, feed themselves. Because the singularity of a being - neither "matter" nor "spirit" -, it is perhaps that very thing that it must invent to get out of a montage of its memory. To escape from this infernal trick of illusion. It is not a question then for him to *represent* the ways that he discovers, but to follow them. To be *in* the real because *it becomes again* the real. The unforeseeable of an impulse.

Then the true nature of eternity and infinity is revealed: they were only childhood memories[171]. The memories of a love without limits.

WHO are you?

"Who are you?" And she, without hesitation, "I am the wandering soul."

André Breton, *Nadja*.

"The service you can do me is to believe that all the earth is only an immense rigged theater, a Châtelet of

---

171. Proust, as always a precursor, when he evoked his mother's kiss, wrote: "[...] when she had bent her loving face towards my bed, and had held it out to me like a wafer [...]", Marcel PROUST, *Du côté de chez Swann*, in *À la recherche du temps perdu*, t. I, "Bibliothèque de la Pléiade", Gallimard, Paris, 1991, p. 13.

5. Listening/dreaming. Therapeutic track

black magic that the fools do not want to see and that the scoundrels of the initiated conceal as long as they can."

Antonin Artaud, "Letter to Colette Thomas," March 27, 1946.

Who associates? Certainly not the "I".

The answer is perhaps to be found in the very *movement* of the associations, where something *is being* lived, to *be* found through affects that have been forgotten until now. To recreate oneself by finding a path. An ephemeral language, ignored, that everyone can however, by instants, understand: *the Esperanto of the dream.* The language of the third kind. The one that one can only speak for a time, that one forgets when the day comes.

"The mind is the idea of the body", this mysterious Spinozian statement then becomes clearer. The being of the memory is indeed something like a "body", virtual body certainly, associative, but more real perhaps, more singular in any case, than the actual body, the body of flesh and bones. And *the affectivity, the sensibility of the memory*, is the sensibility of this body, its own *style*, its unique way to defend itself against all the montages of which the other, each time, inevitably affects it.

Then, torn identity card, disarmed mirrors, "to be" takes a new meaning. If affects are paths of memory, we *are* these paths.

To exist: inimitable *movement*, differing[172], which assumes and goes until *deploying* a difference. What protests: "I am not that [...] nor that [...]"[173], dismantling all the definitions, refusing all the hierarchies, the anguishing roles where the world of the value tries to incarcerate it. To be, it is *the singular form that this refusal can take. Determinatio negatio est,* says Spinoza. The universality of a rebellion. The strength of a "No!

---

172. The *a* that marks a pain and an audacity. A cry. Everything that Heidegger dramatically lacked to *differentiate* himself from Nazism. Heidegger to whom however Derrida refers when he comments on his neologism: "The *Différence*". A neologism to be treated derridianly, therefore without deference. And without hesitating to *differentiate* from it.

173. "An individual acquires a true proper name, at the end of the most severe exercise of depersonalization, when he opens himself to the multiplicities that cross him from side to side, to the intensities that run through him [...] There was my meeting with Félix Guattari, the way in which we heard each other, completed each other, depersonalized each other, singularized each other, in short, loved each other", Gilles Deleuze, *Pourparlers*, Minuit, Paris, 1990, p. 15-16.

At the moment when the *double secret* of anguish has been pierced, a new dimension opens up. Neither space of play, nor lost time, but perhaps both at the same time. Something else. Winnicott *and* Proust. What makes us live again, if only for a moment, our *dingularity*, this unknown party, the bursting of all the assemblies, the possible found. The eternity. Another scene.

This could be the stake of the theater where every evening, in full light, in front of hundreds of eyes, tightrope walkers of the affect risk their life. Making all the arrangements of their own history waver, thwarting these tricks of illusion, actors reinvent their roles.

Conclusion - The Double Secret

A huge fake theater

The spectator, believing he has discovered the secret of the trick, exclaims, "It's in the other hand..." The illusionist, with a slight smile because having anticipated the remark, opens his empty hand, thus imprisoning the truth in a double turn.

Jean Gabirot, *Psychoanalysis, illusionism.*

The illusionist turns to one of the spectators:

- A magician, in principle, never reveals his secrets. It's because, you see, we live the illusion. Tonight, however... Listen.

The *real* is doubly concealed. It is by tearing off its *two* masks that we have a chance to access it. To be content with revealing the unconscious - a hidden child - is to risk ignoring the world of value, the inexorable social struggle in which this child is unwittingly engaged. Conversely, to be satisfied with revealing this unknown is to leave anguish, the cause of all violence, the source of all Terrors, unchecked.

This mutual concealment, the secret of the secret, constitutes the essential of the trick. If I am breaking the professional ban of illusionists by revealing it to you, it is because, I know, you will never talk about it to anyone. You will understand why later.

Wait a minute.

You are, sir, my best companion. Because *I* am another, and without the immense but reasoned disruption of all the *senses*, the transmutation of all the *values* that I propose to you - after Rimbaud, this teenager who was so close to discovering our secret -, it is impossible for you to understand it.

To explain the trick, I will have to repeat the different times.

At the beginning of the show, we turn off the lights in the room. Darkness is essential for the projections. So you thought you were sitting in this room watching me and all my props on stage. You were wrong. I was indeed on the stage, but you were also there, without knowing it. *Around my eyes, your memory was wrapped,* it framed them; you did not see it, it is however it which manufactured my glance. The magic of my gestures, that of my words, was only a creation of your desire. Your appetite for wonder - this great breath that had swept through your memory before enveloping me in enchantment - emanated in reality from an image of yourself, long ago, in the time of the powerful magicians, your parents. This ancient image was revived by the impressive nobility of my bearing, my peremptory talk, this wand, my golden robe. These mythical attributes that diverted your attention, you did not recognize them.

Every person, every object, everything was, in the dark, invisibly cut in two by a concept crystal partition. On the one hand, your conscious operations made my hat flutter to hang on a word, a prize. In other ways, this hat, now a piece of cloth, was traveling in your past before finding itself in one of your dreams.

There was no more separation between stage and hall. Only one immense childhood: yours. Your story, in which - a bit like a huge thumb, a monstrous tongue are projected on the bark of your brain - a giant but invisible childhood took almost all the space, a virtual reality where soft and authoritarian women reigned.

If you had let your associations come however, this childhood, you could have gone through it freely. The only way to take back your own memory from the powers that always try to reduce it, to *edit* it. To maintain a being prisoner of this assembly which anguishes it.

A violence, to which we must oppose the insurrectionary force of the metaphor, nothing better has been invented to beat everyone, even the light. The courage of creation, the energy of the dream: the art of resisting the word of the dominant, this masked imposture. In short, never give up this slightly crazy desire, this project that nothing, no power will ever succeed in killing: *to be*.

The real, finally, would have circulated then. You could have put your finger in the corners, there would have been no more dust here as in the cave of Mr. Plato.

But you didn't do that.

And the lights came back on. In the dark, you were on the stage. You did not move, yet you are now sitting in the room again. A motionless movement, nothing but sense flowing and hiding. Leave my hat on, sir, you'll get your fingers stuck. Don't cling to me, stay in your place. A bit of attitude, please.

Now you can see that everything is back in order. You will again be able to say without laughing: "I, I…"; you will be able to speak about your "inner life", to oppose it to the "external world". You will again be fooled by the illusion trick.

What you take for reality is back in place. You will never again ask the hidden question, the question of *value*: "Who is in charge?" Perhaps fleetingly you will question the *meaning*. You will get no answer. You will then be a little afraid, without really knowing why. These questions are not good to ask.

The rose has gone under the cement. Marx does not wake up the world any more. Rouletabille has forgotten the perfume of the lady in black. Oriane de Guermantes has left us. Citizen Kane has stopped looking for *Rosebud*. Did you know that Orson Welles, the magician-monster, initiated to illusionism by Houdini, had spent the night before his death doing card tricks?

I am not afraid that you will betray my secret, I said.

You see, *forgetting is part of the trick.*

You now get up from your seat. You put on your coat. You are going to leave the room, go back to the street, go home. You look hurried again, a little worried, a little annoyed. Your everyday look. The normal air.

You forgot.

One night, however, something will come back from this lost moment. It is a dream that will bring you the precious certainty: another assembly is possible.

Another montage.

From the same author

Novels

Nuit blanche avec reflet fauve, Flammarion, 1992.

La machine à déplier le temps, Flammarion, 2000.

News

La qualité du silence, Denoël, 1997.
Gérardmer/Fantastic'Arts literary jury prize.

Tests

The mask and the dream, history of the unimaginable, Flammarion, 1994.

"Letter from Sigmund Freud to Karl Abraham" in En pays lointain, collective work (M. Gribinski, dir.), Gallimard, 1994.

Heidegger, Primo Levi and the Redwood. La double inconscience, Gallimard, 2001.

Psyche Prize 2002.

LA SYNCOPE DE CHAMPOLLION. BETWEEN IMAGES AND WORDS, Gallimard, 2003.

"LA CHAMBRE DES ENFANTS TERRIBLES. UNE MUSIQUE DE FILM" in PARLER AVEC L'ÉTRANGER, collective work (F. Gantheret and J.-B. Pontalis, dirs.), Gallimard, 2003.

WHAT AN OVERWHELMING LITTLE SENTENCE IN THE HEART OF A BEING? PROUST, FREUD, SPINOZA, Gallimard, 2005.

"I IS A CASE: WOLFSON" in DOSSIER WOLFSON OU L'AFFAIRE DU " SCHIZO ET LES LANGUES ", collective work, Gallimard, 2009.

DREAM STRUGGLE AND CLASS INTERPRETATION. DISMANTLING A TRICK OF ILLUSION, L'Olivier, 2013.

Table

Best sellers Max Milo Editions

Hitler's banker, Jean-François Bouchard

Confessions of a forger, Éric Piedoie Le Tiec

The Koran and the flesh, Ludovic-Mohamed Zahed

Governing by fake news, Jacques Baud

Governing by chaos, Collectif

A political history of food, Paul Ariès

Mad in U.S.A.: The ravages of the "American model",
Michel Desmurget

Mondial soccer club geopolitics, Kévin Veyssière

Putin: Game master?, Jacques Braud

Treatise on the three impostors: Moses, Jesus, Muhammad,
The Spirit of Spinoza

TV Lobotomy, Michel Desmurget

www.ingramcontent.com/pod-product-compliance
Lightning Source LLC
LaVergne TN
LVHW051156060726
842526LV00014B/3227